Here's what people are saying about Susie and Otto . . .

"This book is a tool I will recommend to people who come to me seeking help with their own questions of whether to stay or go. As a workbook, it is a great adjunct to counseling, helping to reveal to clients what they may already know about themselves as well as where they are stuck a͟   ͟ help."
                    –Belinda Gore, Ph.D., The Enneagram I͟   ͟tral Ohio

"Thought provoking, stimulating, inspiring and pro͟   ͟ook will give you lots to think about. It will help you dig a ͟   ͟help you to make a better choice about staying or leaving a r͟   ͟en you are ready to make this choice … read this book! W͟   ͟the Collinses. You must take the first step while you are still a͟͟
                    –Larry James, Author, Professional Spea͟   ͟Relationship Coach

"Susie and Otto Collins are two authentic, life partners who share from their hearts and, more importantly, model what it truly takes to create an outstanding relationship. Through personal stories, a wide variety of books and practical ideas, they offer new possibilities for creating and sustaining the love we want in our lives. I recommend their work and appreciate their grounded generosity."
                    –Kathlyn Hendricks, Ph.D., Co-founder of the Hendricks Institute
                                        for Conscious Living

"I just wanted to thank you for giving me such great advice. I wrote you four months ago, and at the time, I was so scared when I left my husband, and you gave me so much courage to push forward. I am so glad I did leave. My life has changed around. It's not perfect, but considering what I was in, it is fabulous now. I have found out so many things about myself. I even started treating myself better and I have even learned how to forgive him and stop hating him."

                                        –Cynthia Jeans, North Carolina

"Your information and tools provided in your tapes and books have been very valuable for me in transforming my relationship. Over the past few years I have read numerous relationship books to help me have a wonderful, passionate relationship. Nothing compares to your books."

–Sue Afrasiabi, Melbourne, Australia

"I would like to sincerely thank you for the wonderful job you are doing. I look forward to my newsletters via e-mail. They are short and sweet, to the point and really make you think about what's important in your life. I have printed every one and saved it in a 'special personal folder' for myself."

–Michelle Liporto

"I have been receiving your newsletter for many months now and I am always ready to read and apply your insightful messages. It is very encouraging to realize my personal growth in some areas and look to new approaches in others. As I read, different relationships pop into my head, those, of course, that apply to the topic or example — sometimes my mother, then maybe only a sentence later and it's my children or my ex-husband. In any event, it is a wonderful check and balance to take a moment out of each week and look at these relationships that are the most important aspects of our lives. So, I wanted to say 'Thank You!' You have a loyal reader."

–Rhonda McEwen

"I always look forward to the newsletters, like a little treasure chest, filled with golden booklets."

–Dorena Caprice

"A quick note to share my gratitude for your sharing. I have a private practice where I use many modalities to assist people with improving the quality of their lives. Knowing I am unable to be a 'master' at everything, I use your infos and hand them out — they make such a difference! We discuss how the topic may be an area of improvement … and it also serves as a great reference."

–Glenda Gibbs

Should You Stay
or
Should You Go?

Compelling Questions to Help You Make
that Difficult Relationship Decision

By Susie and Otto Collins

Conscious Heart Publishing
Chillicothe, Ohio

First printing 2003

ISBN 0-9725130-9-4

Published by Conscious Heart Publishing,
Post Office Box 1614
Chillicothe, Ohio 45601

Contents

Acknowledgments

We are very grateful to Linda Blaine, Amy Phillips-Gary, Nancy Stewart, Molly Morehead, Suzanne Roberts, Donna Strong and Mark Pitstick for their continued support and valuable contributions to this book. We honor and appreciate all the people who gave us permission to use their stories in the hopes that their words will be helpful in your decision-making process.

We would also like to acknowledge the people we consider to be our teachers. Their wisdom and knowledge has contributed greatly to our personal and spiritual growth, as well as our knowledge of relationships and how to do them differently. Gary Zukav, Kenny and Julia Loggins, Gay and Kathlyn Hendricks, Belinda Gore, Charlotte Kasl, Eli Jaxon-Bear, Stephen Covey, Tony Robbins, Marianne Williamson, Karla McLaren, Don Riso and Russ Hudson, Stephen and Ondrea Levine, Jerry and Esther Hicks and the teachings of Abraham, Patricia Joudry and Maurie Pressman.

In addition to the knowledge we have gained from these great teachers, we would like to acknowledge our own intuition, inner wisdom, love for each other and our path together in spiritual growth.

We would like to thank Vaughan Davidson for the cover concept, Peri Poloni for the cover design, Janice Phelps for interior design and Sonja Beal for editing. Our thanks also go to Mark Victor Hansen and Dan Poynter for their advice and inspiration.

Foreword

What can be more satisfying to a therapist than the opportunity to work with people who are willing to honestly pursue the answers to the most challenging questions of their lives?

That is what keeps me excited about working with my clients and makes my work fresh after many years as a psychologist. That is also what describes my experience in working with Susie and Otto Collins as they individually faced their own dilemmas of whether to "stay or go."

Both Susie and Otto, in their individual journeys, were willing to look at the reality of their respective marriages and to discover the uncomfortable answers to many of the questions posed in this book. Because they were each able to pay attention to their feelings and to honor the spontaneous awakenings and insights that occurred in the process, each of them found reliable inner guidance that helped them make the right decisions and find their ways into a new life and a new relationship — with each other. During the months that led to their decisions to go, they learned a lot about themselves. As a result they were able to build their new relationship on a solid foundation of clear understanding of their individual needs, wants, values, hopes and strengths. It was a pleasure for me to be able to share in their joy in finding each other and to support what evolved as their passionate commitment to each other and eventually to helping others who are also ready to have relationships that fulfill their deepest heart's desire.

The current data tells us that one of every two marriages ends in divorce. Some people use those figures to make pronouncements about the moral decline of our culture. However, some of these so-called "failed" marriages are the consequence of a different kind of radical shift that is taking place in our society. The values of honest communication, a commitment to lifelong learning and the development of conscious living have begun to pervade the thinking of a larger social group. Marriages that were based on a desire to satisfy cultural pressures, lust, insecurity, or the unconscious tendency to follow in our parents' footsteps (even when we protest that we are doing just the opposite!) begin to falter.

There is a growing belief in some sectors of the populace that it is right and good to insist on a new kind of marriage. In this new climate more people are requiring that their marriage commitments be to living, maturing relationships. This new kind of marriage is one in which both people are awake to their own true natures and are committed, sustaining authentic rather than automatic interactions for the course of a lifetime. Sometimes people discover that the partners they chose in their twenties cannot be the partners they need in the later years of their lives. They often realize that they married someone much like one of their parents and that they are reliving the relationships they grew up with. When those parental marriages were troubled or dependent, they very often find someone or something to help them continue the story until they can resolve those dysfunctional relationships. One day a realization may dawn on them that living with an abusive or unfaithful spouse is not the best they can do for themselves. They may find that substitute fulfillment through work or children or sports or shopping is not the inevitable lot of middle age. When that is true, they have to find ways to leave their marriages.

Other couples discover that a shift of perspective into greater awareness and more honesty — with themselves and each other — can revive their present marriages. They find that the old roots can be nurtured to develop new ways of being together that will sustain them.

Neither choice is inherently right or wrong; the important factor is the willingness to pay attention to a marriage that has either gone flat or has become an endless source of strife or discontent.

As a therapist, I am always happy to find tools that can support the process of self-discovery. Financial circumstances and the strong value that insurance companies now place on brief therapy often require clients to find ways to supplement their sessions with a therapist. In many ways this can be a positive factor to help people take more responsibility for uncovering the deeper issues they are facing and developing their own resources to support ongoing personal change and healing.

This book is a tool I will recommend to people who come to me seeking help with their own questions of whether to stay or go. As a workbook, it is a great adjunct to counseling, helping to reveal to clients what they may already know about themselves as well as where they are stuck and need help. It has been my experience that when all the puzzle pieces of a person's life are dug up, cleaned off, and set out on the table, the next step is no mystery at all but is clearly evident. At that point I can mirror the truth that is revealed and support the process of taking action based upon it.

In *Should You Stay or Should You Go?*, Otto and Susie Collins are sharing valuable insights that were tried and found true in the crucibles of their own lives. If you have picked up this book, you are undoubtedly searching for answers to the same questions they have faced. In their relationship coaching practice they have helped many people find their way through a difficult passage. I recommend the wisdom and experience condensed in this workbook as a light that can help you find the next steps in your own journey.

Belinda Gore, Ph.D.
The Enneagram Institute of Central Ohio
www.enneagram-ohio.com
November 1, 2002

Introduction

If you are reading this book, you are probably in the process of making one of the most difficult decisions that you may ever have to face in your life.

We know how painful making this decision can be. In our relationship coaching practice, we've heard hundreds of stories from people who are struggling with this question of "should I stay or should I go?" The process is never easy. We know from personal experience because in previous relationships we have both been faced with making the decision of whether to stay or go.

Otto was married to his first wife for 15 years. The first years of their relationship were great but the last few were filled with challenges and difficult situations that they both had to deal with. As a result of having different goals and visions for their lives, Otto began to grow increasingly unhappy. His ex-wife said she was perfectly happy and thought things were going along just fine up until the point when he decided to leave the relationship.

Otto had never told her that for years he had felt their relationship wasn't what he wanted. One incident was the breaking point and he decided he wasn't going to live like that any longer. He had already planned on attending a weeklong workshop alone, so he used that time to reflect on his situation. The day after coming home from the workshop, Otto told her that he was leaving their marriage.

Otto made the decision to leave based entirely on a vision of what he wanted in his primary relationship. After his week of reflection, he felt that even though he still loved her, she couldn't or wouldn't be the kind of partner he really wanted.

After Otto told her he was leaving the relationship, she asked him if there was anything she could do to get him to stay. He said, "Go to counseling with me," and she said, "I can't do that. I don't want to tell everything about our lives to a total stranger."

Her response further convinced him, and his mind was made up. He had made his decision about what he wanted in a relationship and was willing to do whatever was necessary to have it.

Otto made his decision from his core feelings and from his authentic self, but because both he and his first wife were unable to break from old patterns and beliefs, divorce was a very painful process. We believe that there is a better way to go through life than screaming, fighting and resisting. We believe this also applies to the process of deciding to stay in or leave a relationship.

Otto made his decision to leave his marriage consciously, even though he and his wife had been unconsciously moving through their marriage for many years.

Susie's first marriage of thirty years came to an end after years of both people knowing that the relationship was dying a slow death and both refusing to acknowledge it. There is and was deep love between them, but their different paths and goals widened the distance between them. The initial decision to separate was made unconsciously. But over several months, with the help of a counselor, there was an attempt to take a conscious, honest look at their relationship and what each of them wanted in a partner and in their marriage before they decided to divorce.

We don't believe that every troubled relationship has to end in divorce, as each of ours did. Both of us were in relationships where we didn't consciously express our true and core feelings. At that time, we didn't have the skills or the trust in our partners to make positive changes. Our partners also didn't desire the kind of relationships that we wanted.

If you truly want to make the "right" decision as to whether to stay in a relationship or leave, you need to be as conscious as possible in your decision-making process. The advantage of making the decision consciously is that it allows you to make it with no regrets and with as much ease as possible.

Making this conscious decision isn't easy and we know it. That's why we have written this book. As you read through the process and move into awareness, you will find it easier to examine your relationship and clarify your next steps — whether those next steps are to reclaim your relationship and make it better, or to devise a plan to leave the relationship with grace.

The questions, stories and insights in this book are not intended as counseling or advice about your decision to stay or leave, but rather to provide a powerful process of self-discovery to help you come to your best decision. This process will help you clarify what's going on in the relationship and will allow you to take the time for introspection to discover the answers that have always been inside you.

In this book, it is not our intention to suggest what is right, wrong, moral, immoral, or to pass judgment in any way about what someone should or should not do in their relationships, although we do give our opinions and insights about some of the issues. These decisions are yours and yours alone. Our intention is to present questions, examples and ideas that will help you to gain the insight that you need to make the best, most conscious decision possible when deciding whether or not to stay in your present relationship.

If after going through this book you do decide to leave your relationship, we advise you to make no move for two weeks unless you are in an unsafe situation. If it's a good idea to leave the relationship at the end of this process, it will still be a good idea two weeks later. Take the two weeks and make absolutely sure that this is the right decision for you.

Many people resist talking to a counselor, but a good counselor or coach can help clarify choices, even if only one partner attends. We recommend consulting with a professional counselor or coach, whether you stay or leave, and a lawyer if you need legal advice.

Moving consciously through life can be a joyful, enriching experience and even the process of deciding whether to stay in or leave a relationship can be peaceful and filled with love. We're here to help you in this process.

How to use this book

We suggest that you use the questions and information as a workbook or guidebook. We recommend that you answer all of the questions in the spaces provided, in the order that they appear. Skip only the questions or sections that are irrelevant to your situation. We recommend that you take your time so that you do not feel overwhelmed. If you find yourself becoming overwhelmed, stop and take some deep "belly" breaths. Try to relax and come back to the process later. If you still find yourself overwhelmed, you may want to consider contacting a psychotherapist or coach to help you work through this process.

At the end of each section of questions, we will remind you to breathe and relax to help you to stay centered throughout this process. This is important because when you are living with the question of whether to stay in or leave a relationship, very often your emotions get stuck in your body. When you are stressed, afraid, or sad, you breathe very shallowly in your upper chest. This shallow breathing keeps you stuck and in a "fight or flight" mode. Breathing slowly and deeply, like a baby does naturally, allows you to begin feeling your emotions again without having that feeling of being overwhelmed. Deep "belly" breaths bring oxygen into your body to keep you healthy and calm so that you can make the most conscious, clear decision possible.

We will also give you a positive affirmation to consider after each section. Affirmations are simple words or phrases that when embraced within you, give you a more positive feeling about yourself, your situation, and the possibilities for your life. If these affirmations resonate with you, we suggest that you say them several times throughout the day to remind you to open to the possibilities in your life. They may seem unreal or impossible at first, but if you continue to work with them, you may find that they will help you to shift from your stuck place more easily. In our experience, using affirmations brings a calmness, strength, confidence, and courage if needed to whatever situation you apply them and that's why we have included them in this workbook. Feel free to use these or create your own to help you gain a deeper sense of empowerment while going through this process.

To help you formulate your plan to move from your present state of indecision, we are also asking you to write down steps that you may want to consider along the way. These "steps" could be insights that you get as you answer the questions or positive things you might consider doing either now or later on. Asking you to consider steps at the end of each section is not meant to pressure you to take any action when you aren't ready to do so. This is merely an opportunity for you to write down some thoughts that you have while your answers are fresh in your mind. Remember, this is *your* process. We are here to serve as your guides.

If you and your partner are able to work through this book together, answer the questions separately on paper and then spend time together sharing your answers with each other. Whether you and your partner are able to work on this process together or you are trying to make this decision by yourself, we think you'll find these questions, stories and insights extremely powerful.

The stories in boxes headed by *"Here's How I Made the Decision to Stay in or Leave my Relationship"* are from real people who have agreed to share their thoughts about their decision-making processes. They have requested that their names be withheld to protect their privacy.

These stories have been included, not to influence you one way or another, but to show you how other people have acted in their situations and to give you "food for thought." In reading the stories and examples, we ask you to suspend judgment and assigning blame. We ask you to listen to these voices with an open heart so that insights you need in making your decision will come through. While most of the personal stories are about heterosexual, intimate relationships, this process applies to any type of relationship.

1: Begin Where You Are

Take as much time as you need to answer these questions. Be sure to answer in writing and as deeply and honestly as possible.

1. Why are you considering leaving this relationship?

_____

_____

_____

_____

_____

_____

2. Now we would like to take you deeper and have you ask yourself —
   Why are you really considering leaving this relationship?

_____

_____

_____

_____

_____

_____

_____

_____

_____

_____

3. If you and your partner were able to heal the issues that you listed in #2,
   would you want to stay in this relationship?

   _____

4. Why or why not?

   _____

   _____

   _____

   _____

   _____

   _____

   _____

   _____

   _____

   _____

*Take a break and a few deep belly breaths
to relax. Then ask yourself, "What step(s), if any,
can I consider as a result of answering the
questions in this section?"*

Affirmation

I am willing to look deeply and honestly at my relationship.

❦ ❦ ❦

Notes . . .

2: *Identifying Your Values, Goals and What's Important to You*

People who are in an unhappy relationship often "lose" themselves and their goals and values as they try to deal with challenges with their partner. It's only after you truly know what's important to you in your relationships and your life that you can begin to make conscious decisions about how you want to move forward.

Conscious decisions are ones that are based on your predetermined set of intentions, values and goals. Being aware and listening to your core feelings will guide you to making your decisions in alignment with your intentions, values and goals.

In trying to decide whether to stay in or leave a relationship that's important to you, one of the most valuable things you can do is to identify **your** values, goals and intentions for the relationship and your life. If you are truly honest, you may be surprised to find conflicting ideas, values or beliefs within yourself and with your partner.

Since we are all individuals with differing experiences and outlooks on life, it is perfectly "normal" for us to have different values and goals. Differences are inevitable but if you want a relationship that is alive, connected and growing, there has to be some common thread of values, beliefs and goals that hold you together and keep you growing together as unique individuals.

Not only do we face challenges as a result of conflicting goals and values with our partners, but we may also have conflicting ideas in our own minds about how we want to live, what is important to us, and what we want from our lives and our relationships. These conflicting values and goals within ourselves and with others can be a lot like trying to drive a car with one foot on the brake and one on the gas! You simply can't move forward in your life until you resolve the conflict.

Getting clear about your values

Paul was unhappy with his present relationship and wanted more. After focusing on the type of person he wanted to be with, he met his "soulmate." He believed she was everything he wanted in a mate — she was beautiful, shared the same spiritual growth interest, and had many of the qualities that he thought were most important in a mate. The problem was he was married to someone else and had young daughters, a beautiful home, plenty of money, and a prosperous professional business. After years of agonizing, he decided to stay with his wife. Paul decided to stay, even when his heart told him to move on, because he had conflicting values that wouldn't allow him to leave.

With Paul, there was a values/goals conflict which wouldn't allow him to leave his present situation for his soulmate. He thought that what he wanted most was a close, connected, conscious soulmate relationship, but no matter how hard he tried, he couldn't bring himself to leave his wife and family. He discovered that he valued his role as the family protector, having security, being a good provider, a good husband and father above having his soulmate relationship. He chose to stay and work on his relationship with his wife.

Interestingly, over time, he has discovered a depth, a fullness with his family that he didn't appreciate before. He also can see that part of the soulmate relationship was illusion and projection. He has put more energy into his current relationship and has created a richness that wasn't there before. Realizing what he valued most allowed him to make the decision that he did.

Paul, like many other people, didn't realize what he valued most in life. You can only discover your values when you take the time to discover what's within you.

"Here's How I Made the Decision to Stay in or Leave my Relationship"

"I thought carefully and quietly about what was really important to me in a relationship, what was it that I really wanted, not what my parents and friends would like or approve. I listed my own values and the type of life that I wanted. Then I tried to understand his values and the type of life that he wanted. We both wanted a simple life, harmonious relationship, two kids and a lovely family life. Our important values were very similar. No two people are the same but it's the important things and values that must be similar otherwise it may not work out. For example, if I really wanted kids and he didn't and he wanted to go out with his friends all the time because that was important to him, then that is a major conflicting value. I followed my mind and not my heart and tried to think very rationally about all factors. I didn't want to change him as I shouldn't have to. If you love someone, they should be accepted as they are. Then I realized that my thinking was wrong in certain areas and I was immature in fact. We are now back together and things have been much better than ever. We are truly best friends and whenever issues come up, we just talk about things nicely and gently."

What are your values?

A great way to begin to know what you want in your relationship is to first identify what you really want from your life and to identify your core values.

1a. What is most important to you in your life?
Make a list in the space below and prioritize the importance of the things in your list by putting "1" by the most important, "2" by next, and so on.

_____

_____

_____

_____

_____

_____

_____

_____

_____

_____

_____

_____

_____

_____

1b. Now go back through your list and write down how much time each week you spend with these people or doing these activities. Reflect on the last 2 or 3 weeks and try to give an accurate portrayal of how you are actually spending your time.

_____

_____

_____

_____

2. Take a look at what you say is most important to you in your life. Now take a look at how you really spend your time. Compare the two. Is there a difference between what you say is most important to you and how you spend your time?

_____

_____

_____

_____

_____

_____

_____

_____

3. What is most important to you in a relationship? Make a list of the five to ten most important things to you in a relationship. Put a check mark beside the things that you have in your current relationship.

_____

_____

_____

_____

_____

_____

_____

_____

_____

_____

_____

_____

4. How much time do you spend with your mate every day?

_____

5. Is this enough time to cultivate and grow the type of relationship that you said you wanted and is this a conscious choice?

_____

_____

6. Are you involved in other activities or with other people to avoid, either consciously or unconsciously, spending time with your mate?

_____

7. Complete this sentence: When this relationship first began, the most important things to me in a relationship were:

_____

_____

_____

_____

8. Complete this sentence: Now the most important thing to me in this type of relationship is:

_____

_____

_____

_____

9. Is there a difference between your response to question 7 and question 8?

_____

10. If so, has this shift had an impact on your relationship? How so?

_____

_____

_____

Take a break and a few deep belly breaths to relax. Then ask yourself, "What step(s), if any, can I consider as a result of answering the questions in this section?"

Affirmation

I am willing to be an advocate for myself and the life I really want.

❧ ❦ ❧

Examining Your Personal, Spiritual and Religious Commitments and Beliefs

Personal, spiritual and religious beliefs and commitments are important to all of us. What is essential is that you consciously look at these commitments and beliefs to make sure that they are really your commitments and beliefs and not just something that you "should" believe or do because someone else says so.

Since you, like all individuals, are continually evolving and changing, it's important to make sure that your commitments and beliefs are reflective of the person you are right now and the person you are becoming.

We would encourage you to take an examination of whether your personal, spiritual or religious commitments and beliefs allow you to be happy. By examining your commitments and beliefs, you can determine what will best serve you, your relationship and your personal and spiritual growth. The questions in this section will help you do that.

"Here's How I Made the Decision to Stay in or Leave my Relationship"

"I will start by saying that I was, and still am, a woman who strongly believes in marriage vows. I treasured those words and more than anything, I wanted to be married to this one man for the rest of my life. I guess you could call it the traditional "picket fence syndrome." In addition to this, I am a Christian woman who believes in God's design for marriage, unconditional love and forgiveness. With this as my foundation, I remained in my marriage even though my husband was a compulsive liar, had many sexual dysfunctions and a pornography addiction. My trust level was low from the beginning. The final deciding factor for me to leave came when I stepped back and logically and rationally looked at all my options. I knew without a doubt that I had no energy left to work things out between us. The only question became when would I leave. I was not getting any younger and no matter when I chose to leave, it would be devastating for my daughter. I looked back and saw that I had been living five or six years of my life as a lie. I refused to do that anymore. I wanted to live honestly at all expense. I told my husband everything. I refused marriage counseling and all other alternatives he presented. My mind was made up. He filed for divorce the next day and I never turned back."

How about your beliefs and commitments?

1a. If you were to leave this relationship, are there any commitments you will be breaking with this person?

_____

1b. If so, what are they and how do you feel about this?

_____
_____
_____
_____
_____
_____

2a. What beliefs do you have about divorce and commitment?

_____
_____
_____
_____
_____
_____

2b. Are they yours or someone else's beliefs?

_____

3. Are your religious beliefs influencing your decision to stay or to go? If so, in what way?

_____
_____

_____

_____

_____

_____

_____

_____

_____

4. Do you have the belief that you can't survive, either emotionally or physically, without your mate? Explain.

_____

_____

_____

_____

_____

5. Is this true?

_____

6. Has your partner broken any commitments with you? If so, what are they?

_____

_____

_____

_____

_____

_____

7. Do you believe that unfinished "lessons" or "karma" is keeping you with this person? Explain.

_____

_____

_____

_____

8a. Are you committed to staying in this relationship no matter what?

_____

_____

_____

8b. If yes, if it weren't for your commitment to stay in this relationship no matter what, would you stay in this relationship or would you go?

_____

Take a break and a few deep belly breaths to relax. Then ask yourself, "What step(s), if any, can I consider as a result of answering the questions in this section?"

Affirmation

I am willing to align my life with my core values
so I am able to be who I truly am.

❧ ✿ ☙

Identifying your goals and life direction

Goals and dreams change throughout your life. The goals you have now may be different from the ones you had five years ago. Even if you've never written goals for yourself and think you don't have any, you really do. You just haven't taken the time to identify them as goals. These changing and evolving goals affect your relationships more than you think.

The challenge we all have is to be conscious about our goals. Ideally, we should share our individual goals with our partner and also have goals that we create together. In order for a relationship to really work in a deep, connected way, there has to be what we call "overlap" between the two partners. There has to be some bond, some connection, some ideal that you both share that allows you to build and keep a passionate, connected, alive relationship.

In our relationship, the two of us are very different people. Our "overlap," one of the things that helps us create and keep an incredible connection, is our mutual goal of continuing to grow spiritually and personally. We also have a commitment to help each other in that growth process.

"Here's How I Made the Decision to Stay in or Leave my Relationship"

"I realized our life goals were not the same, not even similar. It has been one of the hardest decisions because we adored each other but we were hurting each other too much by trying to adapt our lives together. Now that we are both with new loves, we are sure it was the best thing to do to split apart. Now we have found new great loves with whom we share a life plan."

What goals do you have?

Take some time right now to answer the following questions because your answers will help you to realize what you want out of life and how you and your partner may want to live in the future. You may find that you and your partner have the same goals in life or you may find that they are radically different.

1. Do you have goals for your future? If you do, what are they? What do you want to be doing in five years? Where do you want to live in five years? In ten years? What lifestyle do you want to be living?

   _____
   _____
   _____
   _____
   _____
   _____
   _____
   _____
   _____
   _____
   _____
   _____
   _____
   _____
   _____
   _____
   _____
   _____

2. Of all of the goals you listed, which are the most important to you? Why?

   _____
   _____

_____

_____

_____

_____

3a. Do you know what your partner's goals are for his/her future? If you
know, write them here. If not, and you feel comfortable, ask.

_____

_____

_____

_____

_____

_____

_____

_____

_____

_____

_____

3b. Are those goals compatible with yours?

_____

3c. If your partner's goals aren't compatible with yours, is he/she supportive
of your goals in spite of the incompatibility and are you supportive of your
partner's?

_____

_____

_____

_____

4a. Do you have goals that you've created together as a couple? If yes, what are they?

_____

_____

_____

_____

_____

_____

4b. If so, are you and your partner committed to these goals you've created together?

_____

_____

_____

Take a break and a few deep belly breaths.
Then ask yourself, "What step(s), if any,
can I consider as a result of answering
the questions in this section?"

Affirmation

I am conscious about the goals and dreams that I have for my life.

❦ ❧ ❦

Notes . . .

3: *Finding Your True Self*

In any relationship that works, there is I, You, and We. In a connected relationship, the objective is to continue to grow both personally and as a couple. You shouldn't have to give up who you are or who you want to be for the sake of the relationship. One of the main causes for relationship breakups is if one or both people in the relationship feel like they are not able to be who they really are within the relationship. In a relationship between two equals, both people are able to find and be their true selves while being with each other.

"Here's How I Made the Decision to Stay in or Leave my Relationship"

"I asked the question, 'Is this relationship making me a better person?' When the answer became a clear no, the rest was just details. Realizing that after four and a half years of marriage, almost eight years of a relationship, and I was not better for it, I knew I had to get out. Having kids made it real difficult to make the decision and to work out the logistics (we still are and probably always will). Now that the relationship is over, it is easier to focus on helping myself grow."

Listening to your heart

With the help of what you have learned about yourself in the sections on values, beliefs and goals, answer the following questions:

1. Complete this sentence — If I could create my life just the way I wanted it, I would:

   _____

   _____

   _____

   _____

2a. Are there any new activities that you've always thought you might like to try if you were not with your partner?

   _____

2b. If yes, what are they and what is keeping you from trying those activities now?

   _____

   _____

   _____

3a. What are some new activities that you would like to try with your partner?

   _____

   _____

   _____

   _____

3b. What is keeping you from trying those activities now?

_____

_____

_____

5a. When you get to the end of your life and look back, what are the three most important things you would like to have accomplished?

_____

_____

_____

5b. Will you feel more supported and feel better able to accomplish the things you consider to be your goals, hopes and dreams by staying in your present relationship or by moving on?

_____

5c. Why do you feel this way?

_____

_____

_____

_____

_____

Take a break and a few deep belly breaths to relax. Then ask yourself, "What step(s), if any, can I consider as a result of answering the questions in this section?"

Affirmation

I am committed to finding and being my true self everyday and in all ways.

❦

Notes . . .

4: *What Are Your Feelings Telling You?*

Now it's time to stop and get in touch with your feelings. So often it's very difficult to see what's really going on in your relationship, but your emotions don't lie.

When you really get in touch with what you are feeling and you know what you are getting out of a relationship, you can better determine whether you want to continue or not.

A great example of this is the story of a woman we'll call Karen. For many years, she has been with her husband who has a drinking problem and is emotionally abusive to her. Although she has thought about leaving the relationship for years, she is constantly working to see the good in him so that she can continue to keep her marriage and life intact. It has been difficult for her to listen to what her emotions are telling her and she tends to become physically sick when the situation becomes unbearable for her. When we asked her what the "payoff" was or what she was getting out of being in this relationship, she searched inside herself and said that she likes feeling needed by someone and enjoys the constant "doing" for a person who cannot "do" for himself.

By acknowledging her feelings and understanding what she is getting out of the relationship, she is listening to her authentic voice. Because she now truly understands the motivations behind her actions, she is better able to decide whether or not she wants to continue the pattern in this relationship.

ıg at your emotions

ıetimes it requires a good deal of effort to uncover what your emotions are trying to get you to see. But, if you take the time to understand what your emotions are trying to tell you, you will have some clear, valuable answers about how to move forward.

1. What are you honestly feeling about your relationship right now?

_____

_____

_____

_____

_____

_____

2. Who would you be if you stayed with this person? What emotions came up for you when you answered that question?

_____

_____

_____

_____

_____

_____

_____

_____

_____

_____

_____

_____

_____

3. Who would you be if you left this person? What emotions came up for you when you answered that question?

_____

_____

_____

_____

_____

_____

_____

4. What would have to happen for you to feel more peaceful, confident and alive in this relationship?

_____

_____

_____

_____

_____

_____

_____

5. What are three specific occasions when you have felt a great deal of joy in this relationship? How did you feel when you were listing these joyful occasions?

_____

_____

_____

_____

_____

_____

_____

6. When, specifically, was the last time you felt joy in your relationship?

_____

_____

_____

7. Do you feel it will be possible to create this feeling of joy in this present relationship ever again? Explain.

_____

_____

_____

Take a break and a few deep belly breaths to relax. The ask yourself, "What step(s), if any, can I consider as a result of answering the questions in this section?"

Affirmation

I am willing to acknowledge my gut feelings
and let them guide me toward what is right for me and my life.

❧ ✿ ❧

"Here's How I Made the Decision to Stay in or Leave my Relationship"

"I was in a relationship for so long, and I was very unhappy. My partner made me feel used and unloved. I used to tell myself that it's all my fault. If I can put more effort, things will be right.

"Unfortunately I was deluding myself. Nothing I did seemed okay as far as he was concerned. One day, I woke up and he said something very hurtful to me. For a moment there, I was completely blank. On my way to work, I thought about it. At work I continued to think about it seriously. I then decided to put myself in his shoes if the situation were reversed. That is when I came to the conclusion that I am out of this relationship. I told myself that I am going to strive to become the very epitome of a strong black woman and I am going to love myself and stop playing a victim."

Emotions that keep you stuck

We have heard it said that emotions can be just like clouds passing through. Emotions can also be a great deal more than that if you allow them to get stuck. When things come up that are difficult to deal with, you have two choices: You can either express them or hide them away and watch them come back up later as unexpressed resentment or anger.

Where are you stuck?

With these thoughts in mind, here are some questions to help you sort out what you are feeling:

1. When you think about your relationship with your partner, what are you most angry about?

_____

_____

_____

2. When you think about your relationship with your partner, what are you most happy about?

_____

_____

_____

3. What does your partner do that drives you crazy?

_____

_____

_____

_____

4. In reflecting on what your partner does that drives you crazy, can you think of any time when you have acted the same way?

_____

_____

_____

_____

_____

5. Would you feel guilty if you left this relationship? Explain.

_____

_____

_____

_____

_____

_____

6. Do you have resentment toward your partner? If so, are you willing to let go of this resentment?

_____

_____

_____

7. Do you feel any regrets about this relationship? If so, what is the regret?

_____

_____

_____

_____

_____

_____

8. Are you being who you really are in this relationship?

_____

_____

_____

_____

9. How does your life feel when you are with your partner? When you are alone?

_____

_____

_____

_____

_____

_____

10. Do you trust your partner? Why or why not?

_____

_____

_____

_____

_____

_____

11. What do you fear is happening right now between the two of you?

_____

_____

_____

_____

_____

_____

12. What do you fear will happen if you stay? If you leave?

_____

_____

_____

_____

_____

13. How are your fears preventing your forward progress?

_____

_____

_____

_____

_____

14. If you are feeling "stuck" and haven't been able to make a decision about staying in or leaving this relationship, what is the "payoff" that you are getting for staying in this stuck place?

_____

_____

_____

_____

_____

Take a break and a few deep belly breaths to relax. Then ask yourself, "What step(s), if any, can I consider as a result of answering the questions in this section?"

Affirmation

When feelings come up, I am willing to express them
in a way they can be heard.

Notes . . .

Notes . . .

Notes . . .

5: Identifying the Real Issues in Your Present Situation

Sometimes it's really difficult to realize what's happening in your relationship unless you're able to step back and get a "bird's eye view," looking at what's going on from a totally different perspective. Often, what you think is the issue really isn't the issue at all.

Separating and examining the major issues that are plaguing your relationship can be helpful in moving you forward to making a more conscious decision about whether to stay or leave. That's what we're asking you to do in this section — to take a deeper look at yourself, your partner and your present situation and see what the issues really are about.

"Here's How I Made the Decision to Stay in or Leave my Relationship"

"There are a ton of complexities of why I left this relationship, but a primary one would be how he kept saying I was 'too . . .' In listening to all the characteristics I was 'too,' I realized that most of these were the things that were the best part of me. I did not mind changing to become better than I was, but being "too intellectual" or 'too intense,' for example, were not things I cared to change about myself. When to leave? When your own behavior is above reproach or truly very close to it, and the other is unaccepting of who you are and disrespectful toward you, and when you find more and more topics of conversation between you as being taboo. I think we forget that relationships are fluid, and when we try to contain them or make them conform to some sort of shape that meets our predefinitions of what's good or acceptable, we're just running our head and heart up against the proverbial brick wall."

What's really going on?

1. What is actually happening right now between the two of you?

_____

_____

_____

_____

_____

_____

2. Have you and your partner made changes or done anything to try to make this relationship work? Explain.

_____

_____

_____

_____

_____

_____

_____

_____

3. If you were to stay in your present relationship, what five things would you want to change about it?

_____

_____

_____

_____

_____

_____

_____

4. What would have to happen for the relationship to be the way you would want it to be?

_____

_____

_____

_____

_____

_____

5. Would you be willing to suggest these changes to your partner? Why or why not?

_____

_____

_____

_____

_____

_____

6. Are each of you willing to do those things for each other to make the relationship the way you both want it to be?

_____

_____

_____

_____

Take a break and a few deep belly breaths to relax. Then ask yourself, "What step(s), if any, can I consider as a result of answering the questions in this section?"

Affirmation

I am willing to explore underneath the surface of my relationship
to see what is really going on.

❧ ❦ ❧

Notes . . .

Notes . . .

Notes . . .

6: *Your Partner*

Here are some questions you may want to ask yourself about your relationship with your partner:

1. What are the three biggest things you get out of being with your partner?

_____

_____

_____

_____

_____

2. What have you learned most about yourself as a result of being with this partner?

_____

_____

_____

_____

_____

_____

3. What are the three things you appreciate most about this person? Why?

_____

_____

_____

_____

_____

4. What do you most respect about your partner?

_____

_____

_____

_____

5a. Do you feel that this is a relationship between two equals and is this by conscious design?

_____

_____

5b. If not a relationship between equals, who is playing the more powerful role and who is playing the more subordinate role? Is this by conscious choice?

_____

_____

_____

_____

5c. If not a relationship between equals and you'd like it to be, what do you think it would take for both you and your partner to feel like equals?

_____

_____

_____

_____

_____

5d. If you could change this dynamic, would you?

_____

_____

6. If you do not choose to leave this relationship, do you think your partner
   will choose to end the relationship? How do you feel about this?

_____

_____

_____

_____

_____

_____

*Take a break and a few deep belly breaths to
relax. Then, ask yourself, "What step(s), if any,
can I consider as a result of answering
the questions in this section?"*

Affirmation

I appreciate my partner and the experiences he/she brings into my life.

❧ ❦ ❧

Notes . . .

Notes . . .

7: *Communication Between the Two of You*

Communication is one of the top problem areas between people in any relationship. The reason that most people have communication challenges is that they are afraid if they say to their partner what they are really thinking and feeling, and acknowledge what's going on inside them, they will destroy the relationship.

If you want to have a great relationship, you have to communicate constantly — not just about the big things but also the small things. We've often said that if it were not for fear, we would all have outstanding communication in our relationships. Unexpressed truth will eventually be far more painful for you and your partner than expressing your feelings from your heart in the moment. When you think you are protecting someone's feelings by withholding your truth, you are really only building walls and setting the stage for fear, assumptions and doubt.

"Here's How I Made the Decision to Stay in or Leave my Relationship"

"I copped out. I used an opportunity to avoid having to really talk about the truth, which I thought would be too hurtful. I left the area for another job and told my significant other that we should use the opportunity for a trial separation. I was so guilty about ending the relationship that even suicide seemed an easier route to take. I cared so much about her, but I knew inside that we weren't right and I had met someone else."

"Here's How I Made the Decision to Stay in or Leave my Relationship"

"I was engaged to a man who was my best friend for three years. He lived in Colorado, while I lived in Ohio. We traveled back and forth for months, and we made the decision that he would move to Ohio, as I am a small business owner. I found out quickly that I had made a mistake. I had not considered 'reality,' which meant looking at 'us'. We were from different cultures, economic status, spiritual points, ages, and just very different places mentally. I agonized for weeks, but after much prayer, I approached him with my truth, which was we are too different, and I knew I had my answer when he told me he wasn't willing to give it time, or space. It had to be his way, or no way. I was crushed. I thought love was supposed to be different. I knew I would lose his friendship as well, but in my heart I knew our 'relationship' wasn't right. He has since wanted to come back, but I stand firm in what my gut and my God tell me. Once I was honest with my self and him, the pain has disappeared. I still pray for him every night."

How do you and your partner communicate?

Take some time now to honestly examine communication between you and your partner.

1. Do you feel safe expressing your feelings to your partner?

_____

_____

2. Is your partner willing to listen to you when you talk?

_____

_____

3. Is there anything you are willing to change about how you relate to your partner and how your partner relates to you? If yes, what?

_____

_____

_____

_____

4. What would you most like to say to your partner if you felt safe enough and free to say it?

_____

_____

_____

_____

_____

_____

_____

5a. Are there topics that you cannot and will not discuss between the two of
   you? If yes, what are they?

_____

_____

_____

_____

5b. Why are you unwilling to discuss these things?

_____

_____

_____

_____

Take a break and a few deep belly breaths to
relax. Then ask yourself, "What step(s), if any,
can I consider as a result of answering
the questions in this section?"

Affirmation

I communicate openly and honestly with the people in my life.

Notes . . .

64

8: Expectations

Unexpressed and unconscious expectations can ruin relationships. We once had a conversation that illustrates this point beautifully with a woman we'll call Mary. She waited with great expectation all day at work for her husband to send flowers to her office in honor of their anniversary. He never did. Instead, he brought flowers home with him to surprise her. The next day, she told her co-workers how upset she was with him and that he had ruined their anniversary because he hadn't sent flowers to her at work. Mary expected flowers to be sent to her at work, but her husband wasn't aware of the "rules" she had unconsciously set up in her mind for celebrating anniversaries. She was upset with her husband but hadn't shared her expectations with him in advance. He never knew why she was upset.

In all of our relationships, we each have expectations. If you want a happy and harmonious relationship, you will want to share your expectations with each other. This way you each know what the rules are for what's important to each other.

Looking at your expectations and those of your partner will help you to identify some of the issues that may be causing you both to feel disconnected and unhappy in your relationship. By taking the time to identify these issues, you will be more conscious in making the decision whether to stay in or leave your relationship.

"Here's How I Made the Decision to Stay in or Leave my Relationship"

"I was in a marriage where in spite of being in it for a long time, long enough to have high school aged kids, I was just not happy. My spouse is a wonderful human being, but as partners in life, there was no real bonding, as there was no communication. Every time I wanted to bring up anything for discussion, it ended up as my problem as he had no problems. In other words, there was something wrong with me. Now for me to say there is something wrong with me is fine but for him to say it, was not acceptable at all.

"Then I went for psychoanalysis, but that did not help as my analyst's response was, 'So, get a divorce.' All along I knew that more than just my life gets affected with the divorce, and I for sure am not going for that. My children are far too precious and special for me to have them go through this trauma. There was no physical abuse or anything but he was just not there for me in anyway when I needed him.

"That gave me a lead, and I decided that come what may I am here to stay. Prayers, yoga with the most wonderful teacher, and my acceptance of working it out all helped me. Through yoga and the themes that go along with it, I realized that the problem is really me. Not that the fault is entirely mine but, yes, I was handling it the wrong way. I had gone into the marriage with expectations to receive all that I had missed in my early years. But I had not gone into it with clear thinking of what I plan to put into it. I wanted to be pampered, loved, cherished, understood, but had not thought of doing the same for my spouse. And anything that he did which I did not like, I wanted him to change, without trying to understand the reasons behind it. So I had not really accepted him for what he was.

"Unfortunately he was not even the communicative type, so he never explained anything. Thanks to the awareness and acceptance of all this, the support of my yoga teacher, and my wanting to make this relationship work, things have changed. I have changed!! And believe me when I gave up wanting to change him, he has changed. Today after celebrating our silver anniversary with God's Grace we have a relationship which we could have started with. We still have our differences and we still happen to hurt each other sometimes, but now it is easier to talk about it and, yes, we communicate."

What are your expectations?

1. What expectations did you have when you began this relationship?

_____
_____
_____
_____

2. Did you and your partner create these expectations consciously together?

_____
_____
_____
_____

3a. What does your partner expect from you in this relationship?

_____
_____
_____
_____

3b. If you don't know, have you asked?

_____
_____

4a. What do you expect from your partner?

_____
_____
_____
_____

4b. Have you communicated those expectations to him/her?

_____

_____

5. Are your or your partner's expectations getting in the way of having the
   relationship that you've always wanted?

_____

_____

6. How does he/she want you to change?

_____

_____

_____

_____

7. Would you like yourself if you changed the way your partner wants you to
   change?

_____

_____

Take a break and a few deep belly breaths to
relax. Then, ask yourself, "What step(s), if any,
can I consider as a result of answering
the questions in this section?"

Affirmation

I am willing to share with the people in my life what would make our relationships more alive and rewarding.

Notes . . .

Notes . . .

9: *Conflict*

Taking an objective look at how the two of you handle conflict in your relationship can be very enlightening. This can reveal a great deal about what's going on in the relationship.

For us, as it is with many couples, old "baggage" comes up for each of us during situations of conflict. In our previous relationships, we both had the pattern of running away, physically and emotionally, when conflict came up.

At the beginning of our relationship, we came to the realization that if we wanted it to work, we needed to gain each other's trust and develop the skills to be able to listen to each other as non-judgmental friends and to work on solutions to disagreements together as a team. We decided that we both wanted a connected, conscious, loving relationship and realized that running away had only caused us separation from our loved ones in the past.

Sometimes there is still the old familiar feeling of wanting to run away when there's a disagreement between us, but we don't do it. Both of us feel that there's far more pain in the separation that comes from the disconnection between us if we shut down our emotions and run than if we stay present and honestly talk over the situation. Because we have a great deal of safety and trust in our relationship, when conflict arises we try to consciously learn about each other and ourselves instead of shifting into attack and blame.

How you handle conflict in your relationship helps determine whether the relationship weakens or grows stronger when conflict arises.

It has been our experience that most people learn to handle conflict from watching how their parents handled the conflict between them. Susie's parents never showed that there was any conflict between them. Disagreements were not tackled honestly between them and were only discussed with trusted friends — if at all. With Otto's parents — Otto's father was in charge and when things didn't go the way he thought they should, his anger would explode. We both learned that it wasn't safe to deal with conflict or show anger. It wasn't until we began to explore healthier ways of relating to each other that we learned to talk about disagreements as they come up and work together to resolve them.

Becoming conscious about your patterns helps you begin to learn to choose healthier ways of dealing with disagreements between you and your partner, which always leads to healthier relationships.

How do you and your partner deal with conflict?

The answers to your questions about conflict can be used to work with your partner to improve your relationship or to help you to move toward the kind of future relationship that you want.

1. When there's conflict between the two of you, how do you react? Do you withdraw? Become combative? Give in?

_____

_____

_____

_____

2. Are you uncomfortable with your reaction?

_____

_____

3. How does your partner react when there's conflict between the two of you?

_____

_____

4. Are you fearful of your partner's reaction? Explain.

_____

_____

_____

_____

_____

5. Do you do things to punish each other in this relationship, such as withdrawing attention, withholding sex?

_____

_____

_____

_____

6. What criticism does your partner most often lob in your direction?

_____

_____

_____

_____

7. What criticism do you most often lob in your partner's direction?

_____

_____

_____

_____

8. Is there any truth to these criticisms?

_____

_____

9. When there have been conflicts in previous relationships, have you reacted in the same or similar ways as you do now? Explain.

_____

_____

_____

_____

10. How do you feel about your answer?

_____

_____

_____

_____

11. Is the way you deal with conflict a pattern from your past that you are willing to begin to heal?

_____

_____

Take a break and a few deep belly breaths to relax. Then, ask yourself, "What step(s), if any, can I consider as a result of answering the questions in this section?"

Affirmation

I am committed to choosing healthier,
more empowering ways of dealing with disagreements
with the people in my life.

Notes . . .

Notes . . .

10: *Identifying Patterns of the Past*

We've heard it said that the definition of insanity is repeating the same things over and over and expecting a different result.

A woman we'll call Sophia has been with three different partners since we have known her and two of those relationships have ended unhappily. The three men she has chosen have very similar physical, mental and emotional characteristics. She keeps choosing the same type of partner, repeating the same patterns, and wonders each time why the relationship didn't work out.

This is what a lot of us do. We continue to repeat the same patterns over and over and wonder why we keep having the same issues come up with different people.

Below are the stories of two people who discovered how the patterns of the past were ruling their lives.

"Here's How I Made the Decision to Stay in or Leave my Relationship"

"My husband was my first relationship. He was a good man, different from the crowd I was used to, and at the time that was all I needed. It is disturbing how easily we fall into the trap of our parent's pictures of ourselves, even when we know them to be wrong. Growing up I had no praise, no encouragement, no display of affection, just the proper way of morning and evening greeting. My soliloquies during my teenage years, promising myself not to raise my children in that environment, fell through - my husband was my father, and I was becoming the victim my mother always was. Too late I realized it was passion I longed for."

"Here's How I Made the Decision to Stay in or Leave my Relationship"

"The interesting thing is that I knew that the marriage wouldn't work because my gut told me so but I thought I could buck my gut instinct and that my Higher Power would fill in the gaps. Sadly, I found out that the Higher Power doesn't work that way. Even sadder is the fact that it was my third marriage and I repeated that same pattern over and over and over. Now, I'm working the 12 Steps in an attempt to clear myself of any mistaken coulda/shoulda/woulda's and I'm finding that forgiveness and acceptance are the most freeing things a person in this situation can give themselves. The sheer fact that we have the right to experience joy and say 'no' to a society that derives much of its energy from angst and control has been a life-changing experience all by itself."

It's important to look at any patterns of the past—whether they are your patterns or your parents'— that you may be continuing to live out in this current relationship. By identifying the patterns that you continue to repeat, you may be able to heal this present relationship or at least gain an understanding about these patterns so that you don't repeat them in another relationship.

What are your patterns of the past?

1. Are there any similarities between this relationship you are considering leaving and any others you've ever been in before? If so, list them.

_____

_____

_____

_____

2. Does this relationship have any similarities to your parent's or grandparent's relationships? If so, what are they?

_____

_____

_____

_____

_____

3. Does your partner have any similarities to your mother or your father? (Dig deep because there is usually something!) If so, in what ways?

_____

_____

_____

_____

_____

4. How do you feel about your answers to the last two questions?

_____

_____

_____

5. If there are patterns of the past that have shown up in this relationship, do you feel that you and your partner will be able to change those patterns to create healthier ways of relating to each other?

_____

_____

6. What would it take to change those patterns?

_____

_____

_____

_____

_____

7. Are you willing to take the necessary steps to heal those patterns and let them go?

_____

Take a break and a few deep belly breaths to relax. Then, ask yourself, "What step(s), if any, can I consider as a result of answering the questions in this section?"

Affirmation

I am willing to let go of the patterns of the past that no longer serve me.

❧ ❦ ❧

Notes . . .

Notes . . .

Notes . . .

11: Love and Sex

The word "love" is so ambiguous and means something different to all of us. Most will agree, however, that love should be the basis of a committed relationship. Identifying the type of love you want and the type of love (if any) that exists between the two of you is helpful when you are considering whether to stay in your relationship or not. Many people considering leaving their relationships say they love their partner but want more. They say there's no spark or passion between them and they just don't know how to recapture it. It is all up to you to decide the type of love that you want in your relationship and whether it's possible to have it with your current partner.

"Here's How I Made the Decision to Stay in or Leave my Relationship"

"He didn't seem to have the things I was 'requiring in a relationship,' so I didn't think it would ever work. I also knew that he pushed a lot of my buttons on things that bothered me about men, such as feeling it was ok to check out other women, even though he was in a committed relationship, pornography, etc. I stayed at first because I told myself it was just going to be temporary and that I would just enjoy the good things about him — his affectionate nature and his ability to appreciate love. I kept reminding him that it was only going to be temporary. He disagreed and thought we did have a chance and that he was willing to do anything to make it work. I didn't want to change anyone ever to what I wanted them to be for me. I told him so, but he said that it wouldn't be changing him. It would be making him a better person. I had a mixture of feeling sorry for him and wanting to give him a chance, and a genuine feeling of being so attached to him after this went on for nearly a year. I felt a lot of love for him and felt I would be cheating myself to be away from him, even though my struggle may be harder for me than it was for him, since I was the one that was not satisfied with how he was and not the other way around. His love and pursuit of me kept me in the relationship. After a lot of patience and compromise on both our parts, we have come to a mature decision to stay committed in the relationship. We've been married for 7 months now and we are moving happily forward in our relationship. There are still struggles, but not ones that I feel we can't work out. I now live for what I do have that I love about being with him, our love for each other, and his affection for me. Sometimes listening to the heart is the right thing to do, but it does probably cause a lot of pain and struggle, but it may be worth it! It was for me."

"Here's How I Made the Decision to Stay in or Leave my Relationship"

"I believe it was my Spirit breaking free of the chains I had put around it and myself. I started to see that Yes — I had a husband; Yes — I had a home; Yes — I had children. These were my dreams. But what was missing was love! What good were any of these things, without Love? I realized that my 'dreams' that I achieved, were only an illusion, a belief system conjured up and followed by society — they were not real. I did not have the two-way loving, caring, sharing relationship with the person that was meant to be my life partner. But — I had children. What was I to do? I had no choice then, but to be really honest with myself for once in my life. And I stopped resisting my nagging thoughts and let them come to the surface. This was when the 'question' popped up. 'Do I really want to spend the rest of my life with this person?' I listened to my gut reactions this time! This was not the person for me. This was a person who was happy to control me. The great shame of it all was that I let him. It took me many years after leaving to realize that I was not a victim of my husband, but that I had attracted him to me, because I lacked the knowledge of my own self worth. So I did it myself! Once I realized that, many years later, I was able to forgive him and let go of all my anger and resentment towards him. I took responsibility for how my life turned out. I asked myself, 'If he had an affair, how would I feel?' When my answer was 'relief,' I then realized that I really had no basis for staying. If I didn't care, and even welcomed him being with other women, then what relationship did I really have?"

When a sexual problem shows up between two people, it is usually a symptom of something going on much deeper with one or both partners rather than the sexual problem itself. It is helpful to identify the sexual dynamics between the two of you so that you can take a deeper look at what's underneath those problems. These challenges that show up in sexual dynamics between two people can be power issues, communication problems, feelings of lack within each person or any number of unresolved issues from the past.

"Here's How I Made the Decision to Stay in or Leave my Relationship"

"In my previous relationship, I had the experience of being impotent nearly all of the time. At those times, my ex-wife would say something like 'You're not as young as you used to be' and I would believe her even though I was in my 30s. When it started happening again in my new relationship, I really began to wonder about myself and if I could ever have sex again the way I wanted it. When it happened the next time, my new partner said to me, 'I'm just going to love you anyway,' implying that she would love me whether we could have sex without the aid of a drug or not. It was then that I made the decision that I could really be with this woman and love her in an unconditional way. Her saying that she would just love me anyway gave me everything I needed to know and built the trust that formed what has turned out to be the most incredible relationship I've ever had. When there is distance between my wife and me, the impotence sometimes returns. But as a result of regaining our connection, impotence no longer becomes an issue for us."

How about love and sex in your relationship?

1. Are you and your partner "in love" now?

_____

_____

2. Do you enjoy talking and being with your partner?

_____

_____

3. Why were you initially attracted to your partner?

_____

_____

_____

_____

4. If you didn't know your partner, would you be attracted to him/her if you were just introduced today by a friend?

_____

_____

5. Do you think your partner is attractive and "sexy"?

_____

_____

6. How important is sex to you in this relationship?

_____

_____

7. How important is sex to your partner?

_____

_____

8. When you and your partner have sex, who initiates it more often—you or your partner?

_____

_____

9. How often do you have sex with your partner?

_____

_____

10. Is this a conscious decision by both of you?

_____

_____

11. Are you satisfied with the frequency?

_____

12. Has your partner expressed that he/she would like your sexual relationship to be different from what it is now? If yes, how?

_____

_____

13. How do you feel about this?

_____

_____

14a. Would you like your sexual relationship to be different than it is right
now? If so, how?

_____

_____

_____

_____

14b. Have you discussed this with your partner? If not, why?

_____

_____

_____

_____

*Take a break and a few deep belly breaths to
relax. Then, ask yourself, "What step(s), if any,
can I consider as a result of answering
the questions in this section?"*

Affirmation

I choose a love and sexual relationship that is satisfying
for both my partner and me.

Notes . . .

Notes . . .

12: *Flirtations and Affairs*

We have a unique perspective on flirting with or having an affair with someone else while you're in a committed relationship. We believe that the only reason that someone would ever flirt with or have an affair with someone other than their committed partner is that their needs are not being met in their primary relationship.

Whether you or your partner is flirting under the guise of having good-natured fun or just being "friendly," there is some unconscious need that's not being met. The same thing goes for having affairs.

We've talked to hundreds of people who are mired in blame and judgment over this issue. They simply can't move past their own pain to realize the truth about their situation — that one or both partners' needs or wants are not being met in the relationship. This may have nothing to do with their current partner but rather it is within themselves. Until the unfulfilled needs and wants of both people are unearthed, it's impossible to create a conscious, connected relationship.

"Here's How I Made the Decision to Stay in or Leave my Relationship"

"I think my biggest unresolved issue is guilt and feeling like I betrayed my husband. I'm a very loyal person but because some of my emotional needs weren't being met, I found someone else to pay attention to me. I didn't persist in trying to resolve or fix my relationship. We just drifted. When I finally confronted my husband, I had a strong connection to someone else who I thought met the needs that my husband wasn't. The things that made me decide to stay were his willingness to work on things and a commitment to go through the book *Relationship Rescue,* by Phil McGraw, together. We'd been together for 25 years and had a lot of memories, shared experiences and two grown children. I'd also seen several couples who were close friends split up and they still had a lot of problems. My husband & I were good together in a lot of ways and I had done a lot of growing in the past 5 years and we'd worked through those changes. We hadn't gotten past a lot of problems and rarely fought. My husband is also a very loyal person and I knew if he committed to work on things that he would.

"That was two years ago and we've had our ups & downs. Mostly ups but he struggled for a long time intermittently with what he felt was my betrayal and his lack of trust in me. I let him feel those feelings and kept telling him I was here to stay. I had to work through several times being myself and not who I thought he wanted me to be or not doing what I wanted because he felt threatened. One of the biggest things that has come of this is my expectations and what I want out of a relationship. I've become a lot more self-assured and I feel comfortable and confident to do things on my own. If my interests are different than my husband's in some areas, we can each do our own things and that's ok. We still do a lot of things together and we care what each other is doing. I used to think that to have a great relationship you had to do everything together after work or something was wrong. I often felt lonely and that something was missing but I seldom expressed that. If I did express it I didn't do anything to try and fix or change it. One of the things I have gotten out of this experience is that I don't need other 'male attention' now as I get that from my husband and I have my own confidence."

Are flirtations or affairs a challenge in your relationship?

As you read in the previous example, flirtations and affairs usually have to do with the search for feeling important, validated, desirable and is not just about wanting "sex" with someone else. While we're in no way condoning flirtations and affairs or blaming the partner who was cheated on, looking beyond blame to the underlying emotional needs that are not being met in the relationship is the path to healing and growth.

If your relationship is or has experienced this challenge, the questions in this section will help you to move beyond blame and judgment into understanding what one or both of you want from your relationship that you haven't been getting up until now. Your answers will help you to decide whether you want to begin the process of rebuilding trust to heal your present relationship or to move on.

If you have ever flirted with other people or had an affair, answer these questions:

1. Why did you do it and what unmet needs within you were you unconsciously trying to fill?

_____

_____

_____

_____

2. Have you told your partner about your unmet needs?

_____

3. Is the flirting or affair still going on?

_____

4. If this was/is an affair, does your partner know about it?

_____

5 If your partner knows what effect has this had on your relationship?

_____

_____

_____

6. If you are having an affair that is still going on, which relationship is more important to you—the relationship with your primary partner or the person you are having the affair with? Why?

_____

_____

_____

_____

_____

_____

_____

_____

If you know that your partner has flirted with other people or had an affair, answer these questions:

1. Is this still going on?

_____

2. How do you feel about these flirtations or the affair(s)?

_____

_____
_____

3. What effect has this had on your relationship?

_____
_____
_____
_____

4. Are you willing to ask about his/her unmet needs?

_____
_____
_____
_____

5. Are you willing to consider making the changes needed to fill those needs that are important to him/her? Why or why not?

_____
_____
_____
_____
_____

6. Would you like who you would be if you made those changes?

_____
_____

*Take a break and a few deep "belly" breaths.
Then ask yourself, "What step(s), if any,
can I consider as a result of answering
the questions in this section?"*

Affirmation

I am willing to explore unmet needs in my relationship.

❦

Notes . . .

Notes . . .

13: *Money*

How you handle money in your relationship will tell you a great deal about the dynamics going on in the relationship itself. Money is one of those "hot button" issues than can be a major challenge in relationships.

One of the most important things to work out as early as possible is the balance of power and vulnerability between the two people. Ideally, both people should be able to be both powerful and vulnerable with each other. Money is an issue that often reveals power and control struggles.

Recently, we met a woman who told us that because she was a stay-at-home mother and her husband made all of the money, he had the final decision on everything purchased in their family. Her role as stay-at-home mom was not valued as highly as his as "breadwinner." In this relationship, the woman's husband holds all of the control and power because of their agreement. We've discovered that when one person holds all of the power and the other is more vulnerable, there's no way to avoid resentment by both people in this lop-sided power dynamic.

Many people believe that if they had more or even less money, their relationship would be better than it is right now. Our experience tells us that that is not the case. Whether a couple or family has a great deal of money or very little money is not as important as whether they are conscious about the agreements they have about money.

"Here's How I Made the Decision to Stay in or Leave my Relationship"

"The ways my partner and I handle money are like night and day. She is a spender and I am a saver. We really locked horns about money issues when we were first married and it was one of the biggest issues that would divide us. Instead of letting our differences about the way we handle money destroy our relationship, we decided to see what we could learn from each other. I decided to consciously let go of some of the fear associated with money and be more of a 'possibility thinker.' (My parents were from the Depression generation) My wife decided to be more conscious in her spending and is even more accepting of the word 'budget' these days. Money was starting to destroy our relationship until we decided to work together on this issue instead of making it a battleground between us. This has made a huge difference in our relationship."

What is your and your partner's relationship to money?

Your answers to the following questions will reveal to you the similarities and differences of how you and your partner look at the subject of money. Your answers to these questions will help you to look at your patterns of the way you've handled money (or lack of money) and bring you an awareness of the power and vulnerability challenges that you both face.

If money is a challenge for you and your partner, these questions will help you to formulate a healthier way of dealing with issues surrounding money in the future.

1. Describe how you handle money and your finances.

_____

_____

_____

_____

_____

_____

_____

_____

_____

_____

_____

_____

_____

_____

_____

_____

2. How did you decide or learn to do it this way?

_____

_____

_____

_____

_____

_____

_____

_____

_____

3. When it comes to money and finances, what is most important to you? Why?

_____

_____

_____

_____

_____

_____

_____

_____

_____

4a. In your relationship with your partner, who has a bigger influence about how money is handled and financial decisions made?

_____

_____

_____

_____

4b. Has this been a conscious decision? Why or why not?

_____

_____

_____

_____

_____

4c. How do you feel about this decision?

_____

_____

_____

_____

_____

5. How are you and your partner different when it comes to handling finances?

_____

_____

_____

_____

_____

_____

_____

6. Are those differences large enough to drive a wedge between the two of you that can't be healed or can you accept these differences and allow your partner to be who he/she is and still stay in the relationship?

_____

_____

_____

_____

_____

_____

_____

_____

7. If you stay in this relationship, how would you like financial matters to be handled in the future?

_____

_____

_____

_____

_____

8. Is this different from the way finances are currently being handled in your household and how important is that to you?

_____

_____

_____

9. Are you willing to discuss this with your partner?

_____

_____

Take a break and a few deep belly breaths to relax. Then, ask yourself, "What step(s), if any, can I consider as a result of answering the questions in this section?"

<u>Affirmation</u>

I choose to be more conscious about how money
affects my relationships and me.

❧ ❦ ☙

Notes . . .

14: Physical, Sexual and Emotional Abuse

If you are considering whether to stay in this relationship or to leave because of potential or actual physical, sexual or emotional abuse, our opinion is clear and definite. Physical, sexual or emotional abuse of any kind in any relationship is unacceptable for any reason. If you are interested in having a loving relationship as a part of your life experience, there simply is no room for physical, sexual or emotional abuse. Unless the abuser wants to change his/her behavior and get the help needed for this change to take place, we recommend that you leave this harmful situation and seek help for yourself, both physically and emotionally. See the appendix for helpful info.

"Here's How I Made the Decision to Stay in or Leave my Relationship"

"I made a decision eight years ago to leave an abusive marriage. When I first met him, I thought he was my knight in shining armor. We married quickly. I became pregnant and the abuse began. I did see red flags before I married but being the great co-dependent I was, I just knew I could fix him. Of course, after many years of counseling and prayer, I have learned that people don't fix people. Abusive relationships were a pattern in my life but I wanted desperately to break the cycle. The birth of my daughter was a big incentive for me to leave the abuse. I did not want her to grow up as I did, seeing her mom and dad argue and fight. With that in mind and a strong faith in God, I left. It probably took about six months to be completely free of him in my life. I didn't think I could live without him. It was terrible withdrawal — like a heroin addict, except I was having withdrawal from an abusive man. I thought I would die without him. I look back now and see how sick I was. I did break free but it was the most difficult thing I've ever done in my life. Leaving him was the best thing that has ever happened for me. I have not met my soulmate yet but I knew that God has taken the past eight years to heal and prepare me for when he does come. Life is good, I have learned to love myself. If I had not left I truly believe I would have died — maybe not literally but mentally I would have."

"Here's How I Made the Decision to Stay in or Leave my Relationship"

"I made the decision to leave a relationship because I knew if I didn't while I had a little self-esteem left, I would eventually lose it all and not have the strength or courage to ever leave and things would only have gotten worse. My boyfriend was raised by an abusive father, both physically and verbally. While my boyfriend had a good heart and was a decent and caring person, because of his abusive past, he displayed abusive behavior towards me at times. He never was physically abusive, although when his temper flared I was frightened that it could turn out that way. When he got angry, he was so verbally abusive that I began to lose my self-esteem. The more self-esteem I lost, the more abuse I allowed because somehow I thought I caused or deserved it. I stayed with it for as long as I could because I kept making excuses for his behavior due to his family background and I felt sorry for him. I felt that someone who loved this person had to hang in there with him so that he could change. I eventually sought professional counseling and told him that if he didn't join me that I was going alone. After sharing some stories of our relationship with the counselor, she advised me that she would not counsel us as a couple because she believed the relationship could not work with mere counseling, but that she would work with each of us individually and that he would have to do a few things such as attend an anger management class as a start. Of course, he never agreed to do this because he blamed me for a lot of his outbursts. He could not see his behavior for what it was. The counselor ended up being right and I realized that the only way you can truly help an abusive person is to not put up with the abuse under any circumstances, which takes an unbelievable amount of strength when you love someone. If the abuser runs out of people to abuse, hopefully he/she will eventually seek help. But, if they can find even one person to take the abuse, the cycle continues. I do believe that verbal abuse leads to physical abuse. I was lucky that I had enough self-esteem left to make the right decision to leave the relationship."

Is abuse part of your relationship?

1a. Are you fearful of possible physical, sexual or emotional abuse in this relationship?

_____

_____

_____

_____

1b. If so, does your partner know about your fears?

_____

_____

2a. Is your partner fearful of possible physical, sexual or emotional abuse from you in this relationship?

_____

_____

2b. Are you sure?

_____

_____

3. Is there violence now between the two of you? If so, give details.

_____

_____

_____

_____

_____

_____

4. Has your partner ever been physically, sexually or emotionally abusive to you in this relationship? If so, give details.

_____

_____

_____

_____

_____

5. Do you have any knowledge of your partner being physically, sexually or emotionally abusive in other relationships in the past? Again, give details.

_____

_____

_____

_____

6. Have you ever been physically, sexually or emotionally abusive to your partner in this relationship or in previous relationships? Explain.

_____

_____

_____

_____

_____

7. Are you willing to stay in this relationship if there is abuse of any kind between you and your partner? Why or why not?

_____

_____

_____

_____

Take a break and a few deep belly breaths to
relax. Then, ask yourself, "What step(s), if any,
can I consider as a result of answering
the questions in this section?"

Affirmation

I deserve to be in a relationship where I am loved
in a safe and respectful way.

Notes . . .

Notes . . .

15: *Addictions*

We have received hundreds of requests for advice from people who are in relationships with partners who have had addictions of one kind or another. The number one comment that's made is that the person thought that his/her partner would change and that he/she could help the partner to make that change. The attitude is that "I just need to be good enough or strong enough or loving enough and he/she will change and everything will be fine."

We're not suggesting that a person can't let go of his/her addictions. What we do know is that being with someone who has addictions brings on a whole other set of challenges to the relationship that usually involves more help than the partner can give. Improving the relationship usually depends on a great desire on the part of the one who has the addictions to get the help that will allow him/her to move forward.

"Here's How I Made the Decision to Stay in or Leave my Relationship"

"I do know that it's a bad thing when one does not want to come home. That is a sign that things are not going very well. Also, using alcohol and drugs to dull the pain when you have never had a problem before is TELLING YOU TO DO SOMETHING! It's time to evaulate your situation!"

"Here's How I Made the Decision to Stay in or Leave my Relationship"

"About six years before the divorce was final, I had started going to counseling because I felt that there was something wrong with the way I had been feeling toward my husband. He seemed happy and I wasn't. I just knew that the problem was me, but the relationship felt like we were just going through the motions in everything we did, like there was no substance. I thought I had communicated to him how I was feeling, but what he heard and what I meant were two different things. He seemed to never really listen to me though. Several months into counseling, I began to realize there were many issues in our relationship that were to be resolved with both of us working with a counselor if we were going to make this marriage work. I asked him if he would start coming with me to sessions. He had a drinking problem, and I finally realized I didn't want to deal with those issues anymore and mine as well. Our kids were getting older and I noticed they would worry about their father being out on Friday night when he wouldn't come home right after work. I couldn't do that to them and it was up to me to stop our behaviors toward the drinking problem. He showed up a few times to talk with our counselor, but not on a regular basis at all. The counselor told me that it was ultimately up to me what I wanted to do with my marriage because I couldn't change him. I had gained a lot of weight through the years, which I realize now was so symbolic of me trying to hold myself back from leaving this relationship. You see it had been drilled into my head for years, that if you were divorced God would punish you somehow. You just didn't get divorced. I started reading many books on spiritual growth and healing. I wanted to make sense of how completely confused I was feeling toward God, toward my husband and toward myself. I didn't even understand or know who I was any more! I finally started praying and meditating to God to please help guide me to what I needed to do with my marriage. I began to feel it in my heart that if I stayed with my husband, I would be hindering both of our chances for healing and growth. I prayed for my husband to be happy because he deserved it just as much as I did. But most of all I prayed for my children. I did not want them to hurt because of us. Well, sometimes hurting for a short period of time helps us all to grow, too.

"After we decided to separate, the kids were hurt of course, as well as many family members, although we began to see how much better our children behaved and performed in school. My husband and I never fought much around them, yet there was always tension between us. I do believe this was the right decision, but it was not easy."

Are addictions hindering the growth of your relationship?

Identifying and facing addictions in a relationship can be a first step to understanding and facing the reality of what's really going on. Addictions might include drugs, alcohol, food, sex, work and many others. Addictions always point to a deeper challenge going on inside a person. Your answers to these questions can shed light on your "stay or go" decision.

1a. Do either you or your partner currently have addictions that are negatively affecting your relationship? If so, how?

_____

_____

_____

_____

_____

_____

_____

1b. If there are addictions, have you and your partner talked about them?

_____

_____

_____

1c. If you recognize a problem, does your partner realize that this is a problem in your relationship?

_____

_____

_____

1d. Are you or your partner seeking help right now for this problem? If so, how?

_____

_____

_____

_____

1e. Are you or your partner willing to do whatever is necessary to deal with these addictions?

_____

_____

2a. If your partner has addictions, do you believe that you can fix this problem or help your partner change?

_____

2b. If yes, have you been able to do this up to this point in time?

_____

_____

_____

_____

2c. How do you know for sure?

_____

_____

_____

_____

_____

3. If you have any addictions, is your partner trying to fix you? Explain.

_____

_____

_____

_____

4. If your partner has addictions that are causing problems between you, is your commitment to stay with this person more important than your happiness and well-being? If so, explain.

_____

_____

_____

_____

_____

_____

Take a break and a few deep belly breaths to relax. Then, ask yourself, "What step(s), if any, can I consider as a result of answering the questions in this section?"

<u>Affirmation</u>

I am ready to face the reality of the consequences
addictions are creating in my life.

❧ ✿ ☙

Notes . . .

16: *Taking Stock of Other Factors that Influence Your Decision*

Children

We can never be sure how children are going to react, benefit or be hurt by the decisions we make. Even though Susie's daughter Amy was almost 30 when Susie and Amy's father divorced and she understood why their marriage had come to an end, she was still deeply affected by their separation. While the divorce was painful, it allowed Amy and her father to attempt to become closer and get to know each other in a deeper way.

When Otto left his ex-wife, his son was eight years old and it was very painful for both his son and him. It required a lot of effort but Otto continued to have a great relationship with his son even though they no longer lived in the same house. His son naturally had abandonment issues about the situation. Otto simply took one day at a time and continued to prove to his son that he was staying in their relationship even if he was leaving his son's mother.

We are of the belief that we are all here on this earth to experience personal and spiritual growth and we never know how that growth will show up in our lives. In our opinion, whether the children grow up in a home with two parents, one parent or no parents — the most important thing is that they discover how to truly embrace love into their lives. It's also important that they have an ongoing model of real, authentic communication in their lives. One thing we can always be sure of is that children are always better off in situations where there is real, genuine love instead of constant pain and struggle.

"Here's How I Made the Decision to Stay in or Leave my Relationship"

"If I left, then my kids would be products of a 'broken' home. But I also came to understand that staying on just for the children's sake was as damaging to them as it was to my husband and me. They would have been the product then of an 'unhappy' home. Which was worse — products of a broken home or products of an unhappy, loveless home? I grew up in a loveless environment — I knew what that was like. So — if I couldn't stomach the thought of living the rest of my life with my partner, and if staying meant that my children would only learn about how to live in a loveless environment, then I am teaching my children nothing of value for them. If I could be single, and both parents are happy, then they would have two happy homes to be in, rather than being stuck in one unhappy home. So, I decided to grow, and give my children the same opportunity. I believe that staying for the sake of the children is also another outdated myth perpetrated by society. I learned that love is important. And I learned that it's not enough just to love someone else, you have to love yourself too, or there can be no successful, uplifting relationship — with anyone. This is what I wanted to teach my children."

"Here's How I Made the Decision to Stay in or Leave my Relationship"

"I viewed my marriage as a vow and a promise. We've hit a lot of bumps in the road of life and occasionally I get the real sense that things would be easier if we parted ways. This was closest to happening about five years ago — about the time of our son's 'diagnosis.' We both shut down emotionally on anything more than a superficial level and our physical intimacy decreased dramatically at about that time. I have a strong sense of divine order at work in my life and am conscious that I'm meant to stay open to what my creator has in store for me. I've given birth to a unique and amazing child who has given form to my intuitive understanding of unconditional love. There is no doubt in my mind that if my husband & I don't work to stay together and connected and communicating, we will go our separate ways. I came to the realization that a divorced home wasn't the environment I wanted my son to grow up in, and 'giving up' wasn't a behavior I wanted to model for him. Are we soulmates? I guess I'll say that our souls are continuing to grow and mature. I'm grateful for his humor, his intelligence, his support and love for me and our son. I struggle to speak up for what I need; we struggle to find time together in the 'busy'ness of day to day living. As long as we're both trying, we're in good shape."

Children:

Here are some questions for you to consider if children are involved in your decision.

1. Are you staying in this relationship primarily for the sake of the kids? Explain.

   _____

   _____

   _____

   _____

2. Are the children in this relationship aware of the challenges present in this relationship? Why or why not?

   _____

   _____

   _____

   _____

   _____

   _____

3. How would you describe your child(ren)'s current relationship with you and your partner?

   _____

   _____

   _____

   _____

   _____

   _____

   _____

4. How might staying in this relationship affect them emotionally and physically?

   _____

   _____

   _____

   _____

   _____

   _____

5. How might leaving this relationship affect them emotionally and physically?

   _____

   _____

   _____

   _____

   _____

   _____

6. Will the children see a better example of love in action in their lives if you
   stay in this relationship or leave? Why do you feel this way?

   _____

   _____

   _____

   _____

   _____

*Take a break and a few deep belly breaths to
relax. Then, ask yourself, "What step(s), if any, can
I consider as a result of answering
the questions in this section?"*

<u>Affirmation</u>

Each day, I give my children a powerful example of love in action.

❧ ❦ ❧

Your support group

When you are in the process of making the decision whether to stay in or leave a relationship, it's very important that you seek the support and help of other people. You need people you can talk with, to share how you are feeling and what's going on with you now and in the future no matter what you've decided to do.

Susie had a "best girl friend" for over twenty years who emotionally supported her after her husband left their relationship. Susie was also involved in several groups which helped her to make the transition from being part of a couple to being single. She found that doing activities with groups moved her forward in beginning a new life instead of staying in victim-mode and dwelling on a past relationship that had ended.

Before Otto left his first wife, he asked a trusted, long-term friend a very important question about how she saw the relationship between him and his now ex-wife. The answer she gave to his question provided valuable insight and clarity from a totally different perspective than he had considered before. This is the value of your support group. If you are open to it, they can give you keen insights that will make your decision-making process much easier and clearer.

Keep in mind that everyone who is advising you is coming from his/her own perspective and from his/her own life experiences. Most people would never say or do anything to intentionally cause you more pain or make your decision more difficult. But, because they are looking at your situation from a totally different perspective, it is important to understand why they would advise you in the ways that they do. It's also important that you keep in mind that no matter how well-intentioned other people's advice is, the ultimate decision is yours.

"Here's How I Made the Decision to Stay in or Leave my Relationship"

"I knew my home life was unhealthy, so I made a commitment to somehow change the situation. I attended a co-dependency treatment program which was the beginning of my beautiful journey. I learned that I could not change my partner, but I could make changes in my own life. From that point on, I struggled to untangle the past. I sought the help of therapy, began a spiritual journey learning the teachings and ceremonies of my native culture and welcomed the support from family and friends who were ever present. In the meantime, my partner continued living the unhealthy addictive, abusive lifestyle he was comfortable with and I wanted to leave the relationship but I wasn't ready to make that step. The fear of being alone overwhelmed me at times because it was associated with my issues that were being sorted out. I focused more on me, becoming healthy and providing a better life for my children and myself without my partner. Our relationship became a new struggle because we lived separate lives with different interests, separate friends and so on. Our children grew accustomed to having an absent father. Then, for a period of four months I knew it was time to let go of my fear so that I could walk away from a relationship that was stagnant. With the help of a positive, healthy support network of spirituality, family, friends and therapy I realized that I deserved a more fulfilling life with a more suitable partner at some point in my life. It was also apparent that our children deserved a more healthy, balanced home life. It's been two years since we separated. There is no chance of reuniting. Although it's been a journey for all of us, I feel I made the best decision for everyone involved."

"Here's How I Made the Decision to Stay in or Leave my Relationship"

"I finally made the decision to leave when I started to feel more empowered by one of my friends. She knew how miserable I was and convinced me that I would be able to make it on my own. To leave the relationship, I would have to move out. That was the scariest part, I didn't know how I would afford to live on my own as well as be alone. It took three more months of convincing, and one day after a night of horrible arguments, I went apartment-shopping. I could barely qualify for an apartment in a decent area that I would not be scared to live in since I had no rental history, but by chance, the apartment became mine. I truly believe that I would have left the relationship eventually, but it was the power of friendship that made me strong enough to do this. Sometimes in a relationship, a person can be so beat down emotionally that they feel like they are not strong enough to handle life on their own. This is very sad, but I have seen this situation more than once. I currently have a friend in a similar situation and I only hope to give her the strength to move on and make it on her own and hope that she will find true love and happiness."

Who is in your support group?

1. Do you have friends or family who will support you in your decision-making process no matter what you decide? Who are they?

_____

_____

_____

_____

2. Have you let them know about your unhappiness in your relationship? Why or why not?

_____

_____

_____

_____

3a. Have you sought out relationship counseling or coaching to help you in this relationship? Why or Why not?

_____

_____

3b. If you have sought relationship counseling or coaching to help you make this decision, what has been their advice to you in this matter?

_____

3c. Have you followed their advice or suggestions? Why or why not?

_____

_____

_____

_____

4a. Has anyone else been giving you advice about whether to stay or go?

_____

_____

_____

_____

4b. If yes, have they ever been faced with this decision and what did they do?

_____

_____

5. Are there any groups or organizations that would be of support to you as you move forward in your life? What are they?

_____

_____

_____

_____

Take a break and a few deep belly breaths to relax. Then, ask yourself, "What step(s), if any, can I consider as a result of answering the questions in this section?"

Affirmation

I am grateful to the people who support me in my life.

❧ ❦ ❧

Notes . . .

Notes . . .

17: *Getting Clear on Your Financial Situation and Housing Options if You Leave*

Take a few moments and consider your financial options if you were to leave your current situation.

1. How would you be able to financially support yourself and children (if any)?

_____

_____

_____

_____

_____

2. How quickly could you get your hands on enough money to support yourself and your children (if any) in the short term?

_____

_____

_____

_____

_____

3. Specifically, how much money would you need to support yourself until your financial affairs are worked out?

_____

4. How did you arrive at this figure?

_____
_____
_____
_____
_____
_____

5. Where would the money come from?

_____
_____
_____
_____

6. Are you certain this financial support would be available when and if you need it?

_____

7. If you are considering leaving, what steps could you take to protect and separate your finances?

_____
_____
_____
_____
_____

8. Are there joint financial obligations that you would have to deal with? If yes, what are they?

_____

_____

_____

_____

_____

_____

9. What are the possible ways you could financially support yourself?

_____

_____

_____

_____

_____

_____

10. What are some ways you have not explored of financially supporting yourself?

_____

_____

_____

_____

_____

_____

11. Are you willing to possibly change your financial standard of living?

_____

_____

_____

12. Have you contacted a lawyer or other professional about your financial rights and options?

_____

_____

_____

_____

_____

_____

Now consider your housing options if you were to leave.

13a. What would your housing situation be like if you left this situation?

_____

_____

_____

_____

_____

_____

13b. Would this be acceptable for you?

_____

_____

14. What would it be like for you to live apart from your partner?

_____

_____

_____

_____

_____

Take a break and a few deep belly breaths to relax. Then, ask yourself, "What step(s), if any, can I consider as a result of answering the questions in this section?"

Affirmation

I choose to become more conscious and take total responsibility for my financial affairs.

Notes . . .

18: Sorting It All Out

Chances are, you already knew what you needed to do before going through this process—whether it meant being truthful in working with your partner to make your relationship better or leaving the relationship— but you really didn't want to risk changing your current situation because it is familiar. You may believe that the "devil" you know is preferable to the one you don't know. This final section of questions will help you to discover what's really the bottom line so that you will be able to move from your "stuck" position.

1. What are you pretending not to know or are not willing to admit to yourself about your current situation?

_____

_____

_____

_____

_____

_____

_____

_____

_____

2. Are you staying in this relationship for any reason other than love and because you want to be in a relationship with this person? If so, what is that reason?

_____

_____

_____

_____

_____

_____

_____

_____

_____

3a. Has the pain or apathy that you have felt in this relationship overshadowed the possibility of ever having the relationship that you want with this person?

_____

_____

3b. If yes, can you live with what might happen as a result of leaving this relationship right now?

_____

_____

_____

3c. If you can't live with what might happen if you leave right now, can you see a time when you might be able to? Explain.

_____

_____

_____

_____

_____

Take a break and a few deep belly breaths to relax. Then, ask yourself, "What step(s), if any, can I consider as a result of answering the questions in this section?"

Affirmation

I choose to take the next logical step toward my happiness.

Notes . . .

Notes . . .

19: *Taking the Next Logical Step*

Did you ever take that new job, buy a new house, decide to take a chance on something and it just felt right to do it? How do you decide to go on a second date with someone? It just seems like the next logical step after having a good time on the first date.

Right now in your relationship, you are faced with a challenge. You are faced with three choices—you can stay in your relationship and work to make it better, you can leave your relationship, or you can do nothing and stay in your present situation as it is. So the question is: At this moment in time, what is your next logical step?

If you are in a committed relationship that is going through some challenges and want the relationship to improve, the next logical step might be to tackle the issues that are underneath those uneasy feelings. Pay attention to your feelings and allow them to guide you to your next logical step.

Most people allow their lives and relationships to operate out of blame, guilt, judgment and "shoulds" instead of using their positive and negative feelings as a barometer for how they want to live their lives.

Whatever direction you take, start where you are and do something to move yourself forward. When you take the first step, your next logical step will be obvious to you. Don't try to make that big jump that's too difficult for you to imagine. Your "jumps" should look to you as the next logical step. Here are two examples from people who took their next logical steps in their relationships:

"Here's How I Made the Decision to Stay in or Leave my Relationship"

"Tom & I have been married 28 years, and in the past few years I have felt anguished and conflicted about whether to leave. I decided a few weeks ago to move out of the bedroom into a spare bedroom. I didn't realize what a big step this move would be. The second night I was sicker than I had ever been, with chills, pain, and nausea that lasted the entire night. I awoke the next morning realizing that this was no flu. I had been so afraid to take this step that it had literally made me sick! Then I started going to bed early to read in bed, a habit I had always loved but hadn't done for years. I read until late in the night every night, no longer following my husband's alarm and 10:00 curfew. I started feeling more like myself, and realized that I was beginning to feel happier and more alive, just because I had made this small move out of our bedroom. At first, he was hurt, but I explained how important it was for me to have my own bed and that we would both sleep better, since we both snore.

"As a light sleeper, every time I felt Tom turn over, I turned over. I hadn't realized that this unconscious 'synchronized sleeping' arrangement made me feel that I was accommodating him, even to choreographing my sleep to his. I came to understand why I always felt like an underling in the relationship, and the resentment I didn't even know I felt started to lift. Now, we both go to bed early, with each of us reading. Sometimes he visits me in my bed and I visit him in his bed, and we talk about our day, our plans, our son, all the things that we share. We are even talking comfortably about things we never talked about before — things that matter.

"I don't know at this time if I will stay or go, but moving into my own room was a tiny step with unforeseen impact. I now have the space to open myself up to possibilities I haven't even considered, including living across the hall from a man I love and haven't been able to leave."

"Here's How I Made the Decision to Stay in or Leave my Relationship"

"After weeks of deliberation and soul-searching by us both, I decided to leave the family home. I knew I would be going back into my biggest fear, the nightmare of living alone in a small room, etc. I also thought I was failing again. What pushed me to go was the feeling inside that I had spent so much of my life trying to love someone who would not, could not return my love. It was like trying to fill a cracked sink. Half of me gradually realized I would be better off facing the depression than face the agony of this loveless marriage any longer. In the weeks before we split, we went through the process of discussing what it would be like for us both apart. Every day brought a new emotion of loss for us both. I began to realize that my wife loved me. We both spent hours crying in each other's arms. We needed to be apart, also, if not just to find breathing space from the emotional rollercoaster ride of being together. My wife kept saying 'We can't live together or be apart.' So we decided to meet in six months and assess the situation. If we both agreed, we would get back together again. This agreement allowed us to make the break. I think we were kidding ourselves though. Things just started to happen. I went through the process of finding somewhere to live, etc, and moved out. When I got settled into my new, smaller home, I gradually realized that I was not sad or depressed at all, quite the opposite. I felt liberated and eventually became so much more of a real person. I didn't realize how much I had changed, how much more mature I was now. I beat the pain of the split with finding new hobbies and friends, and by facing it and going through it. I also began to realize that being on my own was a special experience; I began to engage in the most important relation-ship of my life, with myself. I still see my ex. We still share an embrace or two. We have both become aware that life has so much to offer, that parting is really just a beginning of something new, and exciting. We had our time together; there was no going back. We are both much happier and more fulfilled people now."

What is your next logical step?

Your next logical step should make sense to you. Below are some ideas to help you begin:

- To ask your partner to go to counseling with you

- To tell your partner that you are not happy

- To take an assessment of your financial situation

- To talk to other people who have made this decision themselves

- To talk to your partner about ways to make your relationship better

- To recommit to your relationship

- To do nothing right now because it isn't the right time but decide to reassess your situation in a month

- To begin to do something for yourself like take a college course

- To take some time for reflection alone about this situation

- To make contact or create a support group that can help you

- To make an appointment with a counselor, coach or lawyer for yourself

- To make your children aware of what's going on with you and your partner

- To begin writing "morning pages"—recording your thoughts everyday—as suggested in the *Artist's Way*

- Schedule a weekly "date" with yourself to do something you've always wanted to do—like paint, ride a bicycle, take a yoga class, dance in the living room

- Schedule a weekly "date" with your partner to do something that you both like to do

- Schedule time each week to talk with your partner—just the two of you with no television

As a result of going through this process and answering these questions, the only question remaining to be answered is, "What is your next logical step in your relationship and life?" Listen to the guidance from within and you can't make a mistake. Write your next logical step below:

_____

_____

_____

_____

_____

_____

_____

_____

_____

_____

In the words of one of our contributors:

"I believe that we get what we give in life. We are a sacred part of creation and we each have the power to make healthy changes in our life if we want to. Our connection with our Creator is the most important relationship we will ever have because through this, we are loved with all there is and ever will be. We are love, we are life, we are sacred."

We hope this process has been helpful to you in making your decision whether to stay in or leave your relationship. Please let us know how else we can help you.

Blessings and love,

Susie and Otto Collins

Appendix 1:

6 Keys to Help You Heal,
(Whether You Stay or Go)

By Susie and Otto Collins

It is very easy to get into a relationship, but when the relationship begins having major challenges, goes sour and you don't know what to do, then your decisions become much more difficult.

Whether you decide you want to stay with your partner and begin working to revitalize your relationship or to move on, here are some strategies and ideas to help you move forward in a more empowering way.

It seems that everywhere you look, many long-standing relationships and/or marriages are troubled or dissolving. If you're like most people, when this happens, you find yourself stuck in thinking about the past, wondering what went wrong, and unable to move from the pain of the relationship. It doesn't matter whether you leave, stay or were left — one of the best pieces of advice we can give you is to leave the past behind and not carry old "baggage" into the new life you would like to have.

We have each been through the break-up of a major, long-standing relationship and have come to appreciate those times in our lives — even though both divorces were very painful. We each, in our own ways, learned how to begin healing by not burying our feelings, and to start moving toward what we wanted most in our lives instead of living in the past. It's this information, plus the experience of working with many people in our coaching practice who were in similar circumstances, that we'd like to share with you.

If you've been living with the question of whether to stay or go for any length of time you have undoubtedly experienced a great deal of painful feelings surrounding the challenges of this relationship.

The problem is, when conflict and challenges come up in most relationships, people tend to react in one of three ways:

Fight, Flight or Freeze.

You've probably heard these words many times before but for most of us, just being familiar with these words still doesn't stop us from going into these patterns when things get difficult.

163

We've learned that most people go into fight, flight or freeze to protect themselves against painful feelings that are difficult or impossible to experience at the time they are happening. But, the problem is many people get stuck in this mode.

These fight, flight, or freeze defense mechanisms are useful sometimes in our lives but if you want to begin the healing process and create close, connected, alive relationships, you have to be willing to explore what you are feeling and have the courage to change this reaction.

For us, we think that the goal is to be so conscious and aware of what we are feeling that when we get triggered by what someone says or does, we are able to simply express what we are feeling without fear, judgment or blame and without jumping into past patterns.

Fight, Flight or Freeze can manifest in a number of different ways. All three of these reactions stem from the fear that your wants and needs won't be met.

Fighting doesn't necessarily mean putting on the gloves and throwing things at each other. Fighting can mean anything from holding onto the need to be right, staying stuck in your anger, holding on to the desire for validation and to be understood, or yelling, screaming and what you think of as fighting. Fighting is holding your ground with your "rightness" no matter what.

Fleeing (flight) doesn't only mean running away physically. It most often manifests as withdrawing emotionally to protect yourself so you won't have to speak or feel painful feelings and emotions. Fleeing can be turning on the television, eating or going to visit a friend instead of dealing with the situation. When you flee or run from what's going on emotionally or physically, the issues are there and won't go away until you come back and deal with them.

Freezing means getting stuck and not being able to move from the impasse of the situation. Very often we freeze because we don't know what to do next, don't have the confidence in our abilities, in ourselves, or in the belief that our life situation will be different beyond this moment. Many people who are frozen and are feeling stuck in their situations have adopted the belief that it's better to deal with "the devil you know" than "the devil you don't know." Because of this, they stay stuck right where they are in situations they are unhappy with and which do not serve them.

To move from the fight, flight or freeze reactions, we suggest that you learn to tune into what you are feeling in each moment and embrace those feelings, whatever they are. When you focus on your feelings, you are not pointing fingers at someone in your past or your current relationship. You are just looking at the situation as it is, and when you do this, you quit pointing fingers and the healing process can begin.

When you find yourself reacting in one of those three ways with the people in your life, stop your normal pattern and reaction, recognize what it is you're thinking and feeling and begin the process of healing the conflict between the two of you.

No matter how much fighting, fleeing, or freezing seems to be serving you in the moment, the undeniable truth is that when you are stuck in any of these patterns, it is impossible to begin creating close, connecting, alive relationships with the person you are now with or someone else as long as you remain stuck.

It's important to learn from the past but it's equally as important to not stay stuck in it. Whether you have decided to stay or go, you have to move forward as if you are starting fresh with a brand new relationship. We're about to share with you the six keys that we find are the most important to help move you from your past to healing, and start you on your way to creating a new, more vibrant life.

Key 1: Never look at a relationship (or anything else) as a failure

Often it's the seed of a current or past "failure" that fuels you to the very success that you've always dreamed of. It sounds trite, but there's always something you can learn from every experience.

Past relationships give you a clearer picture of what you want and what you don't want in a relationship, if you take the time to examine them. It's the power of contrast that living in an unfulfilling relationship may give you.

A woman we'll call Connie brought her intimate relationship to an end after several years of turmoil with her partner. After the break-up, she realized what this relationship had taught her and that it wasn't a failure. This relationship had helped her to define the type of partner she would really resonate with — someone who was on a similar spiritual path, someone she could have a deep connection with, and someone who loved to be with groups of people.

This partner who she left wanted to always be alone with her and she liked to be with people. They also did not have the same spiritual interests, which created distance between them. She learned to bless the relationship and let it go to make room for the type of partner she wanted to be with and to free her previous partner to find a more appropriate mate. She learned that her relationship wasn't a failure because of what it taught her about herself and her life — what she wanted and what she didn't want in a relationship.

People come and go in our lives. Some people are with us for a brief instant, for five months or for fifty or more years. The impact of these relationships on our lives can all be great. Sometimes we don't understand why we are involved with someone in a particular relationship or why someone has such a hold on us. We don't understand why someone comes into our life for a brief time and then leaves.

What we've learned is that if a relationship isn't working out, it is not a bad thing or the failure that our society likes to label it. It just may be that you have learned what it is that you were supposed to learn by being in a relationship with that other person and it's time to move on to other lessons.

We're not suggesting that you take your relationships lightly and throw them away at the first sign of conflict — quite the contrary. What we are saying is that the purpose of all relationships is to help us to grow — personally and spiritually. Even the relationships that are the most troubling to us can be gifts in learning more about ourselves. Those people who really get under our skin can be our best teachers. We suggest that you look at all of your relationships as growth experiences and move forward consciously by learning from them.

So instead of looking at a relationship, that didn't work out the way you had hoped, as a failure, look at it as growth experiences and move forward consciously by learning from them.

Key 2: Turn from the past and look toward the future ...YOUR future

Sometimes after a separation or during the process of rebuilding a relationship, we find ourselves dwelling in the past, our thoughts consumed with that other person. You will begin to heal when you start thinking and writing about what you want for your life.

After Susie's husband of 30 years left their marriage, she found herself thinking about him, wondering how he was doing and if he was happy. It wasn't until she decided to stop focusing on the past and her ex-husband's life and start focusing on what she wanted, that her life began to move forward in a powerful way. It was almost a physical sensation of turning her body forward toward her future. She began to create new goals for her life and pushed past the fear of being alone.

Setting goals is very important in this process of turning to your new life. The famous motivational speaker Zig Ziglar said that he had never met a truly depressed person who had goals for his/her life and we know that this is true. Take some time right now to create some new goals for your new life. What have you always wanted to do? What activities have you always wanted to try but something kept you from trying them? Are there any groups that you have wanted to join? We've found the key to moving forward in your new life is to figure out what you want your new life to look like and you can start small — but start.

166

Here are some things that can help you move forward:

• If you or your partner left your relationship, remove photos of your past partner that are prominently positioned in your house. (You don't have to destroy them. Just put them away.)

• If you're staying in the same house that you and your partner shared, move the furniture and put some different things on the walls. Different inexpensive items that are "you" can really help you to move from your past into your present and future. Even if you are revitalizing your relationship, clear out some clutter together and you won't believe how that will help.

• Sign up for a class that will get you physically active — yoga, Tai Chi, martial arts, aerobics, swimming, tennis. Get your body moving! When you get your body moving, endorphins are released into your bloodstream that help you to feel more positive and uplifted.

• If you are on your own, find a support group — people who will not support you in being a victim or rehash why you left, but groups who will stimulate you into new thought and new ideas.

• If you are revitalizing your relationship, taking a class together at your local university, church or community center can help steer you in new directions together. Also thinking about setting and implementing new goals for yourselves and for your relationship will create movement which in turn creates healing.

Key 3: Know and understand that there are no "accidents" and that everything happens in divine order

Every thought, every moment, every action, every relationship and every event that happens in your life, happens to propel you toward your next phase of learning and personal growth.

Recently, Otto had a conversation with someone that he couldn't get out of his mind. In this conversation Otto was telling this person about some challenges he was having in his life. This person told him that when things in your life aren't making sense and you are confused and frustrated, understand that when you get to the end of your life and look back, everything will make perfect sense.

We thought this was a great way of looking at relationships that didn't work out the way we'd hoped or planned. Sometimes we don't understand why we are involved with someone in a particular relationship or why someone has such a hold on us. We don't understand why someone comes into our lives for a brief time and then leaves. Then there are other relationships that we might have our entire lives — some good, some not so good. The point is that at the end of our lives, if we take a conscious look at our relationships, every one of them will have served us in our growth in some form or the other.

Before we came together, Otto had a relationship with a woman that, although lasting only a few months, had a dramatic effect on his life. He didn't realize it at the time but later completely understood the purpose of that relationship. After the relationship with this person was over, they both completely understood that her role in his life was to be a bridge.

This relationship gave Otto the vision of what was truly possible in a relationship, something he wasn't able to experience with his first wife. Even though this relationship was very brief, had he not met this person, he would not have been ready to create the incredible relationship he now has with Susie.

So instead of looking at that relationship as an accident and one that didn't work, he looks at it as a blessing from God and is thankful everyday for what she gave him.

In one of our workshops, we asked the people in the group to consider the following questions about a person who had come and gone in their life:

• What did I learn about myself by being in a relationship with this other person?

• How did it help me to move forward and heal, learn and grow?

• What new beliefs did I take on or let go of as a result of being in a particular relationship?

As a result of considering those questions, one man in the workshop beautifully described a new revelation about his wife's lengthy illness. He now realized how his wife's illness of many years helped him to grow spiritually and as a person.

We invite you to consider those questions about your partner who has either come and gone or is still in your life. Your answers to these questions may bring an "ah-ha" moment for you too and bring a new appreciation for that person, what you learned by being with that person and what he or she has brought to your life.

Know that every person who comes into your life — whether for five minutes, five years or 50 years — can be a powerful teacher for you if you will only open yourself to the possibility and know that there are no accidents.

Key 4: Take 100% responsibility for the relationship — no more and no less

When a relationship experiences challenges, very often we want to assign fault and blame. When you are in a healthy relationship with another person, both people are equally responsible for the relationship. If a relationship isn't working, the same thing applies. No matter who appears to be at fault when challenges come up, both people are responsible. If you are taking more than your share of your responsibility for the relationship not working out the way you would like, you are being a martyr. If you take less than 100% responsibility for the relationship not working out, you are being a victim. You can only heal when you have let go of fault and blame and focus on letting go of the past and how you can do it differently in the future.

This can be a very difficult process if you are hanging on to the need to be right, anger, judgments and unexpressed resentments — especially if you feel your partner hasn't or won't take any responsibility for the health of the relationship.

Forgiving and forgetting may seem to be beyond reality for you now. It's like if someone says to you, "Don't think of the color blue," "Don't think of the color blue," "Don't think of the color blue." No matter how hard you try, you probably can't stop visualizing or thinking about the color blue.

The same thing happens when you try to forget a negative situation that has an emotional charge to it. No matter how hard you try, you just can't seem to do it. We believe that instead of forgiving and forgetting, you have to forgive and let go.

Many people write to us wanting to know how they can forgive when they have been wronged — a spouse cheated on them; they've been abused in one way or another; or maybe their feelings have been hurt and they don't feel loved or valued. We have found that the process of healing oneself when a relationship has ended or when a relationship is given a second chance requires more than forgiveness. You must also let go.

But let go of what?

In almost all cases when you are having a difficult time forgiving someone, you are holding on to an attachment of some kind or another. The attachments most commonly manifest themselves in the need to be justified, the need to be honored, the need to be right, the need to be vindicated, the desire for revenge, and the inability to move past fear.

So when you are holding onto an attachment, what you are actually doing is holding onto a position which is serving you in some way but it is not moving you forward in healing the relationship. We suggest that you let go of negativity and attachments by deciding to drop them — by deciding that you no longer want to carry and live with the pain and suffering.

Key 5: Learn from the patterns of the past. Stay conscious in all your relationships so that you won't repeat the same mistakes

One woman we know is trying to do it differently after several relationships that ended. She is opening her heart to the possibilities of having the type of relationship that she has wanted but has somehow, up until now, eluded her. She is starting a new relationship without expectations and is just focusing on being real, authentic and true to herself. She's not playing any of the roles she's played in the past as she enters this relationship. There is a different feeling within her about this relationship because of it. She is letting go of some of the destructive ways she has interacted with other partners in the past.

This is the first relationship in which she has been honest about whether or not she wants to go somewhere with her partner. In the past, she would always agree to go wherever her mate wanted to go because she wanted to please him rather than please herself. After doing this for a period of time, she would lose sight of who she was and what she wanted, and resentment would build. Now, she is just allowing herself to open to the possibility of something wonderful happening and being herself in the relationship.

We suggest that the first step in healing any pattern that is a challenge for you or causing you pain is to become aware of what you are feeling within your body when you are experiencing the issue. Susie had the pattern of not speaking her truth when there was conflict in past relationships. When she and Otto came together, she wanted to stop that pattern because unspoken words and feelings would always turn into resentment and create walls with her previous husband. She became aware that she felt a fluttery, sick feeling in her solar plexus and stomach when she didn't speak her truth and held back words. With Otto, she came to recognize those feelings, honor them and allow herself to speak the words she was holding back.

The first step to creating any change is awareness and allowing yourself to notice what's going on in your body — whether it's tightness in your chest, neck pain, headache or nervousness in your stomach. Go back in your mind — when did you notice you would have these sensations in previous relationships. Susie traced her feelings and inability to speak her truth to her childhood. Ask yourself, where did this feeling come from, who was there and what was the situation?

In a new relationship, as well as any, it's very important to differentiate what has happened in the past from what is happening now. Your feelings can guide you to uncovering your patterns and to creating healthier ways of being in your relationships.

Step 6: Give thanks for the lessons that you learned and change your attitude

Haven't many of us been told or maybe we've learned that relationships were hard and filled with misery? We're here to suggest that it doesn't have to be that way. You can decide to have the relationships that you want and to make up your own state of mind.

As painful as it is to hear, the truth is that everything in your life (including your relationships) is a result of the choices you have made. If you don't like the circumstances in your life or relationships, decide to make other choices.

This could mean changing your attitude. It can mean focusing on what you like about your partner instead of what you don't like. It could mean opening up to bring new people into your life. It could mean deciding to be a better person in your relationships.

Whatever your challenges are, only you can decide to take one step forward toward having the relationships and the life you want. If you are having challenges moving on from your previous relationship, we suggest you start by honoring that person as a teacher, here to help you on your journey. When you find yourself feeling the victim or blaming the other person, change that thought to love and send it to him/her. Sooner or later you will actually be able to give thanks for the lessons that that person taught you.

Giving gratitude for your relationship and your life, whether you have stayed or left, will be positive movement to what you want in life. Change your attitude and you will change your life.

Finally, if you would like to heal your life and your relationships, we have a new philosophy you may want to adopt. This philosophy is called "Up until now..."

What the "Up until now..." philosophy means is that no matter what mistakes you feel you've made, challenges you've had or problems you've encountered along the way, today is a new day and anything is possible from this moment forward.

One woman we worked with expressed her concern that her relationships constantly turned out miserably. She had never been able to create what she considered to be a good relationship and was fearful that this would be the way it always would be.

We told her that this may have been true up until now, but in this moment, she had the opportunity to learn to do her life differently. Whether you're twenty, thirty, forty, fifty or eighty years old, it's never too late to begin again.

Whether your challenge is in the area of love and relationships, money, health, overcoming fears or any other challenge, it's never too late to learn a new skill, go to college, take more responsibility for yourself, meet new people, have more fun, make more money or find the love of your life.

So, how do you do this?

Step one is to acknowledge for yourself that there are other people who have exactly what you want for your life and to adopt the belief that if it's possible for someone else, then it's possible for you too.

Once you begin to believe that, yes, other people do have what you want and it's possible for you also to have it, then begin opening yourself to opportunities that will come your way.

Don't beat yourself up if you fall into old patterns that don't serve you. Simply recommit to creating the life or relationships that you want.

If you feel that you must talk to others about your disappointments in the past, always use the phrase, "Up until now.... " By using the phrase, "Up until now...," you are opening your heart and mind to possibilities.

We suggest that when you think you can't have what you want in your life, think of all the people who didn't give up on their hopes and dreams.

If you don't have the kind of relationship or the life that you really want, chances are excellent that there is one of two things standing between you and having what you want — either there are things that you are not willing to do in order to have what you want or you are holding onto beliefs that are keeping you stuck.

We know from our own experience that when we have held onto limiting thoughts and beliefs, such as "I can't... or I could never...," we remained stuck. It wasn't until we opened ourselves to possibilities and changed our beliefs about those situations that we were able to move forward with those goals and heal.

Whether you have decided to stay in your relationship or leave, we invite you to change your thinking, create positive thoughts and affirmations and take some action that will help you to create the life that you want. As you worked through this workbook, you probably thought of some ways to move forward. We now invite you to take this opportunity to move past your fears and start moving toward the relationships and life that you really want.

Appendix 2:

Contact Information

If you are being physically or emotionally abused and want help, call the National (U.S.) Domestic Violence Hotline — 800-282-0530. **The Rape, Abuse and Incest National Network (RAINN)** operates a national toll-free hotline for victims of sexual assault **800-656-HOPE.**

If you need help with alcohol addictions, contact **Alcoholics Anonymous http://www.alcoholics-anonymous.org/.** Yahoo.com allows you to search for AA groups anywhere in the United States from their "Yellow pages."

Al-Anon and Alateen help families and friends of alcoholics recover from the effects of living with the problem drinking of a relative or friend.

For information about drug addictions, go to **Narcotics Anonymous,** http://www.na.org

About Susie and Otto:

We are soulmates, spiritual and life partners, who are committed to helping people like you improve your life and your relationships.

For 30 years, Susie has been a student of relationships, spirituality, energy and the life force. Her search for physical, emotional and spiritual healing has led her to the study of Polarity Therapy, cranio-sacral therapy, reflexology, Hatha Yoga, the Enneagram, and much more. Her formal training includes a Bachelor of Science degree in education, a Masters degree in Library Science, and she is a Registered Polarity Practitioner with the American Polarity Therapy Association. Susie is a veteran teacher and university librarian with over 30 years experience teaching in the public schools and university classes.

Otto has spent over 20 years as a successful salesperson and marketer of a variety of products and services. Many years ago, as a result of pondering three of life's greatest questions — Who am I, Why am I here and What's this all about — Otto turned his life's focus to bear on the practice and study of spirituality, personal growth and relationships.

We passionately believe that life can be lived in a joyful, conscious, loving way and we are committed to helping others to experience the potential of what is possible in their own lives and relationships. The desire to be loved the way we wanted to be loved took each of us on a journey of discovery of how to create the relationship of our dreams. We believe Spirit put us together for our own personal growth and to shine the light of hope for others. Our goal is to help others create outstanding lives and passionate, alive, connected relationships.

Since 1999, we have been creating web sites about relationships, offering relationship coaching, giving workshops and talks, and writing on topics that relate to helping people create vital, alive relationships.

Our free online weekly relationship newsletter reaches thousands of people all over the world. Along with our books and audio tapes, we offer relationship and life coaching to singles and couples in person and by phone.

Our formal coaching training has been with Drs. Gay and Kathlyn Hendricks of the Hendricks Institute and authors of *Conscious Loving* and *Conscious Heart*. We are also ordained ministers through the Healing Angels ministries and licensed by the State of Ohio. We are co-authors of *Creating Relationship Magic* and *Should You Stay or Should You Go?*

For more information about our work or to schedule a relationship coaching session, contact: **Susie and Otto Collins**
www.collinspartners.com   www.soulmaterelationships.com
740-772-2279
webmaster@collinspartners.com

Would you like some help in creating the relationships and the life that you want?

Susie and Otto Collins are available for Relationship and Life Coaching by telephone or in person. Coaching is a supportive way to move forward with your goals and to gain new perspectives on your issues.

For more information about what coaching is and what it can do for you, visit our "Coaching" information page on our website http://www.collinspartners.com.

To discover if coaching is right for you, schedule a free information session with Susie or Otto by calling 740-772-2279 or email webmaster@collinspartners.com.

Discover the Secrets to Creating Outstanding Relationships of All Kinds

Get Susie and Otto Collins free weekly

"Love and Relationships"

Online Newsletter

Visit any of our websites and sign up to start receiving our free online weekly email newsletter. Each week we write a short article on a relationship topic such as communication, trust, jealousy, game-playing, conflict, making agreements, step families and working together. Many people have told us that these short articles have changed their relationships and their lives and we think they can help you too.

By signing up for Susie and Otto's newsletter, you'll also receive regular updates on our latest books, tapes, CD's, teleclasses, workshops and public appearances.

To sign up, go to http://www.collinspartners.com or http://www.soulmaterelationships.com.

Quick Order Form

__ YES, I want_____copies of *Should You Stay or Should You Go?* at $19.95 each, plus $4 shipping per book (Ohio residents please add $1.30 sales tax per book).

__ My check or money order for $_____ is enclosed.

__ Please charge my credit card in the amount of $_____.
__ Visa   __ Mastercard   __ American Express   __ Discover

Name: _____

Address: _____

City: _____

State:_____ Zip:_____

Telephone: (_____) _____

e-mail address: _____

Card #:_____ Exp. Date:_____

Validation Code:_____
        (last 3 digits on the back of your card)

Signature:_____

Please make your check payable to: Susie and Otto Collins

Fax orders: (740) 772-2279
Telephone orders: (740) 772-2279
E-mail orders: webmaster@collinspartners.com
Postal orders:
        Conscious Heart Publishing
        Susie and Otto Collins
        P.O. Box 1614
        Chillicothe, OH 45601
        USA

Printed in the United States
203743BV00001B/107-128/A

9 780972 513098